GW00702119

Korea and Japan

The Clash of Worldviews, 1868-1876

Yongkoo Kim

Korea and Japan
The Clash of Worldviews, 1868-1876

© 2006, Yongkoo Kim

Published and Printed by
CIRCLE
Seoul, Korea

Tel: 82-2-584-3618
C.P.: 82-10-9386-1941
    82-10-5215-3617
Fax: 82-2-584-3617
E-mail: kl5992@netsgo.com
    yongkookim@hotmail.com

First Printing: November 30, 2006
Second Printing: October 20, 2008

ISBN 89-89443-05-9-03340

Korea and Japan

The Clash of Worldviews, 1868-1876

Yongkoo Kim

CIRCLE

BY THE SAME AUTHOR

The Five Years' Crisis, 1866~1871 — Korea in the Maelstrom of Western Imperialism —

Imo Kunran kwa Kapsin Chŏngpyŏn (임오군란과 갑신정변, Imo Military Uprising and Kapsin Political Coup)

Jean Jacques Rousseau wa Kukchechŏngch'i (장 자크 루소와 국제정치, Jean Jacques Rousseau and International Politics)

Sekyeoekyosa (세계외교사, Diplomatic History)

Sekyekwan Ch'ungdol kwa Hankuk Oekyosa, 1866-1882 (세계관 충돌과 한국 외교사, 1866-1882, The Clash of Worldviews and Korean Diplomatic History)

Oekyosa ran muŏtinga (외교사란 무엇인가, What Is Diplomatic History)

Chumchunŭn Hoeŭi — Wien Hoeŭi Oekyo (춤추는 회의 — 빈 회의 외교 — The Congress Dances — A Study on the Congress of Vienna —)

Sekyekwan Ch'ungdol ŭi Kukchechŏngch'ihak (세계관 충돌의 국제정치학, The Clash of Worldviews and International Political Science)

Preface

Diplomatic history is not just a chronology of negotiations between diplomatic actors. It should be based on the theoretical framework of comparative civilizations. This comparative approach posits that there have existed qualitatively different civilizations under which the diplomatic actors' peculiar worldviews, mental structures, or cultural behavioral codes were constructed, developed, and constrained. As such, diplomatic-strategic interactions among the international actors are fundamentally conditional upon the very nature of differences between civilizations.

Through this general historical lens, in this book I analyze the diplomatic relationship between Korea and Japan during the period of the formation of modern nation-states in the nineteenth century. In doing so, three main issues are explored: i) the nature of the Korean-Japanese diplomatic relations institutionalized and stabilized for several hundred years as a peculiar international system; *Kyorin*, ii) how this system was connected to the broader

China-centered international system of East Asia, *Sadae*, and iii) the specific diplomatic processes of the "clash" between the international order of East Asia — *Sadae-Kyorin* — and that of Western international law. The book's central contention is that the current political distrust between Korea and Japan and their heterogeneous perceptions toward each other are historically embedded in their divergent worldviews and deeply rooted in their diplomatic interactions during the formative period, especially the critical eight years from 1868 to 1876. The crux of this historical problem remains largely intact to this day.

The present book is a second installment in a larger project dealing with modern Korean diplomatic history in the perspective of comparative civilizations. The first book was published as *Five Years' Crisis — Korea in the Maelstrom of Western Imperialism* (2002), in which I dealt with Korea's first diplomatic interactions with the Western powers, especially France and the United States, during the middle of the nineteenth century.

In preparing for this book, I am deeply grateful to the late Professor Fred L. Blair for his invaluable comments on earlier drafts. I also thank Professor Ivan Canadas at Hallym University for his interest in the project and his excellent editing. It is my privilege to thank them for their contributions to the accuracy and elegance of this book. It is also my duty to acknowledge the book's many imperfections as my own.

Yongkoo Kim, Hallym University
November 2006

Technical Note

1) All dates in this book are based on the Gregorian calendar generally used in the West. Korean, Chinese and Japanese dates according to the lunar calendar used until 1895, 1912, and 1872 respectively have been converted. Russian dates according to the Julian calendar used until 1918 have also been converted.

2) Korean romanization follows the McCune-Reischauer system. For Chinese, the Hanyu pinyin (漢語拼音, Chinese Phonetic Alphabet, pinyin for short) has been used, except for those names which have entered into common usage by another romanization. For Japanese, Kenkyusha's *New Japanese-English Dictionary*, 4th ed. (1974), a modification of the system worked out by James Hepburn, has been followed. And the transliteration system used for Russian is the Library of Congress system minus the diacritical marks.

Contents

Preface __ v

Technical Note __ vii

Map. Korea and Japan __ xi

Figure 1. Mt. Yongdu __ xii

Figure 2. Taetu __ xiii

Figure 3. Tosŏ __ xiv

Introduction __ 1

1. The Clash between Two International Orders __ 15

2. Korea's New Japanese Policy __ 35

3. Transformation of the *Kyorin* Order __ 57

4. Contents of the Treaty between Korea and Japan __ 79

5. Korea and the Dissolution of the *Kyorin* Order __ 93

6. The Dissolution of the *Kyorin* Order and the Role of the World
   Powers __ 121

Conclusion __ 145

Abbreviations — 149

Bibliography — 155

Index-Glossary — 165

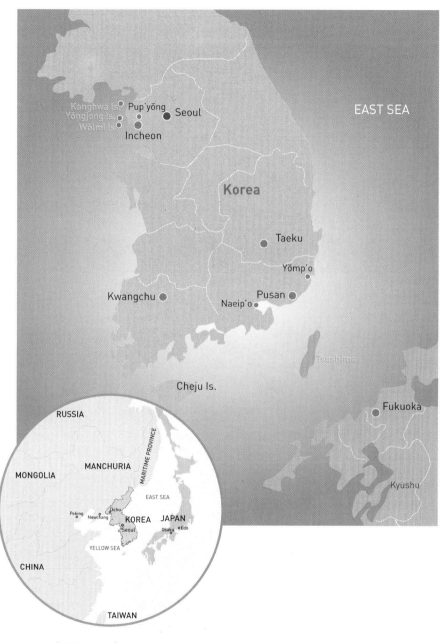

Kanghwa Is.
Pup'yŏng
Yŏngjong Is.
Seoul
Wŏlmi Is.
Incheon

EAST SEA

Korea

Taeku

Yŏmp'o

Kwangchu
Naeip'o
Pusan

Tsushima

Cheju Is.

Fukuoka

RUSSIA

MONGOLIA

MANCHURIA

MARITIME PROVINCE

EAST SEA

Peking
Ŭiju
Newchang
KOREA
JAPAN

Osaka
Edo

Seoul

YELLOW SEA

Kyushu

CHINA

TAIWAN

KOREA and JAPAN

Pusan

Figure 1. Mt. Yongdu(龍頭山), the former site of Japan House(倭館)

Pyŏn Pak(卞璞), Japan House, 1783

朝鮮國王臣李 (名)

欽遇 (年号月日)

元朝令節、謹奉

表稱

賀者、臣 (名) 誠歡誠忭、稽首稽首

上言、伏以

皇帝陛下

為此具本謹具奏

聞、

(年号月日) 朝鮮國王臣李 (名)

謹奉表稱

賀者、[臣]

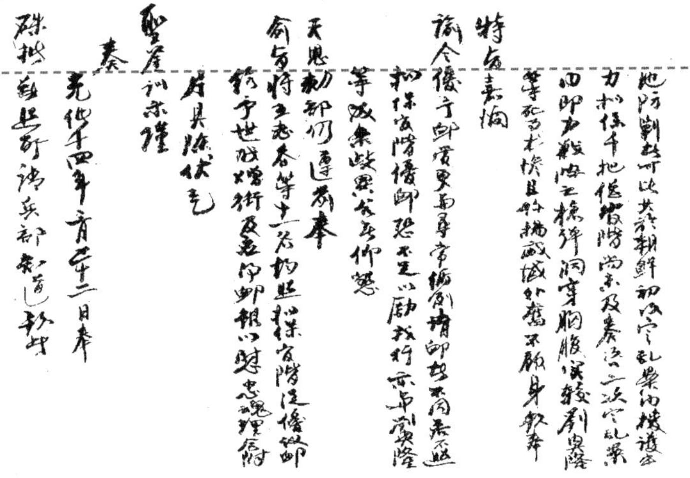

特差嘉猷

諭令優于郎賞更有厚賚編得勸惶有榮遂

抑保宿隣間卿恐至之以勵我行帝中寵隆

等政集歧惡炭成示作懿

天恩勳卿仍連為奉

命与特生忝春卒一等朴堅有隣逗邊節

豹守世成幀術及垕卸卸朝以對忠魂理爵

居具海伏气

聖意示求雅

奏

光化十四年青至二日奉

殊批○此新論兵部知道欽此

三一二

Figure 2. Taetu(擡頭) See p. 11

Figure 3.　Tosŏ(圖書)　See pp.11-12

Introduction

___ Major Agreements Regarding the *Kyorin* Order

___ Tongsinsa

___ *Sŏgye* and *Tosŏ*

___ The Japan House

For five hundred years, from the beginning of the Chosŏn (朝鮮) Dynasty (1392~1910) to the Meiji Restoration (明治維新) in 1868, the relationship between Korea and Japan was regulated by the Kyorin *(交隣, literally, 'dealing with the neighbor') order, which formed a peculiar type of international society between them. As Korean relations with China fell under the jurisdiction of the* Sadae *(事大, literally, 'serving the superior') order, the* Kyorin *order was one of the two main pillars of Korean external relations. Korean-Japanese diplomatic history from the middle of the nineteenth century was, in a sense, a product of the clash between the* Kyorin *order and that of Western international law.*

The peculiarity of the Kyorin *order was clearly reflected in its subject and object. Whereas the Chosŏn Dynasty was a unique and single partner, there were numerous Japanese actors involved in negotiations with Korea. Bakufu (幕府, The Shogunate) in Edo (江戶, nowadays, Tokyo), the Chief Lords of Tsushima (對馬島), and various grandees in the Kyushu (九州) region were regarded as the main Japanese negotiation counter-partners.*

The object of the Kyorin *order was also peculiar. The Chosŏn Dynasty and Bakufu regarded each other as equal actors and dealt with political and cultural matters between the two countries. But the Chosŏn government recognized the Chief Lords of Tsushima and the grandees of Kyushu only as legally inferior partners, even though important economic and commercial relations were conducted among them.*

The trade channel between Korea and Tsushima was especially important to the two partners. The total amount of Japanese silver imported to Korea through Tsushima since the end of the seventeenth century exceeded that of Japanese silver exported to other countries via Nagasaki (長崎). This Japanese silver was used as means of payment for Korean commerce with China. In this sense, the route from Japan → Tsushima → Pusan → Seoul → Ŭichu (義州) → Peking could be described as a 'Silver Road.'

Elaborate rules began to regulate such international relations between Korea and Japan from the early period of the fifteenth century on. Even though there was an unfortunate rupture arising from the Japanese invasion of Korea at the end of the sixteenth century, normal relations were quickly restored in 1609. In these terms, for nearly three hundred years, from the end of the Imjin War (壬辰倭亂) in 1598 until the Meiji Restoration in 1868, the Kyorin *order was maintained rather well between the two countries. But the new Japanese government, following the Meiji Reforms, adopted a new Korean policy. As a result, the continuance of the* Kyorin *order system became an acute diplomatic issue, paving the way for the unfortunate period of modern Korean-Japanese relations.*

Major Agreements Regarding the *Kyorin* Order

When Ashikaga Yoshimitsu (足利義滿), the Japanese Shogun (將軍), was given a patent of appointment as Japanese King by the Ming (明) Dynasty in 1402, Korea and Japan both became members of the *Sadae* order. In 1404 formal diplomatic relations were established between Korea and Japan and thereafter the elaborate *Kyorin* system began to develop from the 1420s.

Because the Korean peninsula was infested with Japanese brigands (倭寇) at that time, the Korean government took the initiative of establishing this international system in order to appease the Chief Lords of Tsushima and the grandees of Kyushu. In the absence of normal trade relations with them, they readily turned to piracy. 'War, trade, and piracy were an inseparable trinity.'

Concluded in 1443, the Kyehae Agreement (癸亥約條)[1] was the first important treaty regarding the *Kyorin* system. The terms of this treaty established the main framework of relations between the two countries. First, a trade system by *Tosŏ* (圖書, seal) was established, similar to the tally trade between Ming and Japan, as will be explained later. Second, actual trade partners were clearly stipulated: the Korean government was the sole actor, although

---

1) CCKJ, Book 4.

there were numerous Japanese partners, such as the Shoguns in Edo, the Chief Lords of Tsushima, Daimyos (大名) like Ouchi (大内), and the grandees of Kyushu.

Among these Japanese trade actors, Tsushima enjoyed the most privileged status. It was permitted to sponsor a fixed number of ships a year (歲遣船), and it was also granted a yearly stipend of a fixed amount of *sŏk* (石, J: *Koku*; one *sŏk* equals 5.119 bushels) of rice and beans (米豆) from the Korean court.

The number of ships and the amount of the stipend were reduced depending upon the behavior of the Japanese side. For example, by the Imsin Agreement (壬申約條)[2] in 1512 after the Disturbance of the Three Ports (三浦亂) in 1510, the annual number of trading ships of the Chief Lord of Tsushima was reduced to 25, and its yearly stipend of rice and beans was also reduced to one-hundred *sŏk*, half the figures previously permitted under the Kyehae agreement.

Nonetheless the Chief Lord of Tsushima was delegated the task of verifying the good intentions of Korea-bound Japanese ships, which had to obtain *munin* (文引, J: *bunin*, a trading permit) from Tsushima officials, a tremendous privilege for Tsushima. However, despite the appeasement policy on the part of the Chosŏn Dynasty, damage caused by Japanese brigands were not completely eradicated, so that finally the Chosŏn court had to seriously consider the Tsushima's role in suppressing Japanese pirates, and to grant Tsushima exclusive trade rights.

---

2) Ibid.

By examining the Kyehae Agreement, one can identify another distinguishing characteristic of the *Kyorin* order: the number of Japanese people who were allowed to reside in Korea and their places of residence were stipulated from the start. The Japanese merchants could only stay in three ports, namely, Pusan (釜山), Naeip'o (乃而浦, nowadays Chinhae 鎭海), and Yŏmp'o (鹽浦, nowadays Ulsan 蔚山). In addition, their number was limited to fifty households. This marked the beginning of the Japan House (倭館). However, the Japanese entrance into the Korean market was increasingly enhanced and the number of her merchants residing in the three ports grew far in excess of that permitted by the terms of the Agreement. As a result, the Imsin Agreement reduced the number of ports of entry from three to one (Naeip'o).

Notwithstanding the dreadful ravages on Korea caused by the Imjin War, normal ante-bellum relations between the two countries were quickly restored. This normalization was due to the persistent effort of Tokugawa Ieyasu (德川家康), the new Shogun, who wanted to uphold his power and to maintain the legitimacy of the Tokugawa Shogunate through the restoration of diplomatic relations with Korea. The Kiyu Agreement (己酉約條)[3] which was concluded in 1609 was the most important treaty regarding the *Kyorin* order between the end of the Imjin War and the Meiji Restoration. It stipulated the three sorts of Japanese negotiating actors, namely the Sogun in Edo, the Chief Lords of Tsushima, and office-holders endowed by the Korean court (受職人). The various

---

3) Ibid.

privileges previously enjoyed by Tsushima were reduced. For example, the annual number of trading ships permitted to its Chief Lords was reduced to 20, but its yearly stipend of rice and beans of one hundred *sŏk* was granted by the Korean court, as fixed by the Imsin Agreement concluded before the Imjin War. The *munin* and *Tosŏ* systems, the most privileged rights for Tsushima, were kept in place as they were before.

But a great change in the *Kyorin* system occurred after the Imjin War. Japanese envoys dispatched by the Shogun were henceforth not permitted to come to Seoul, whereas Korean envoys visited Edo as before.

Tongsinsa

For nearly two hundred years from the establishment of diplomatic relations between Korea and Japan in 1404 to the year of the outbreak of the Imjin War in 1592, the two countries' kings exchanged envoys more than sixty times. But after the Kiyu Agreement the route from Pusan to Seoul was closed to Japanese envoys in the interests of Korean national security. There was good reason for taking this measure: when the Imjin War broke out, Japanese soldiers had easily captured and occupied Seoul within twenty days by following the route from Pusan to Seoul previously used by Japanese envoys. Genbo (玄方), the envoy dispatched by the Japanese king, was the only person to visit Seoul in 1629 in order to exchange information about Ming (明)-

Qing (清) relations in China. This was the only exception.

After the end of the Imjin War, the Japanese kings' envoys sent to Korea on special missions were only permitted to stay in Pusan, where the Korean court would dispatch a 'special inquiring and consolatory official' (問慰使) to receive them. During the years 1607~1868, Japanese kings sent their envoys to Korea approximately fifty times.

But the Tongsinsa (通信使, literally 'communication envoy'), the envoys sent to Japan by Korean kings, were charged with important political and cultural missions. Immediately after the Imjin War, they were called a 'Response Embassy' (回答使), or 'Response and Repatriation Embassy' (回答兼刷還使), but from the time when the Korean embassy was sent in 1636, the terminology 'Tongsinsa' was fixed in its usage. As they were the envoys sent to offer congratulations and condolences to the Japanese kings, as well as for the purpose of solving special problems between the two countries, cordial receptions for them in Japan were stipulated in detail under the relevant regulations.

Tongsinsa were sent to Japan eleven times during the years 1607~1811. The last Korean envoy under the *Kyorin* order sent to Japan in 1811 stayed in Tsushima where the Korean and Japanese delegates exchanged their respective sovereign's messages. By this expedient method of negotiation, the Japanese government and the various *fans* (藩) could lighten the financial burdens of receiving the Korean embassy, which consisted of nearly five hundred men, all along the way from Tsushima to Edo.

Upon becoming Shogun in 1837, Tokugawa Ieyoshi (德川家慶)

asked the Korean court to dispatch a Korean envoy, a request which the Korean government accepted. But on account of Japanese financial difficulties, the whole plan was postponed. In 1853, Tokugawa Iemasa (德川家定) became the new Shogun. Nevertheless the dispatch of a Korean emissary for the purpose of offering congratulations could not be realized, due to an earthquake in Edo and Perry's expedition to Japan.

In 1856 Bakufu (幕府) again requested the Korean court to send a Tongsinsa to Tsushima in 1866, but this also did not come to fruition. Subsequently the two countries agreed that Tongsinsa would be sent to Japan in 1876. But the new Japanese government after the Meiji Restoration of 1868 adopted a new Korean policy designed to change the *Kyorin* order itself. Consequently Korean-Japanese diplomatic relations finally came to a deadlock.

Sŏgye and *Tosŏ*

The formality of the *Sŏgye* (書契), diplomatic documents exchanged between Korea and Japan under the *Kyorin* order, was stipulated in great detail in the relevant regulations concerned. According to CCKJ (See Abbreviations), Japanese envoys sent to Korea by the Japanese kings and by the Chief Lords of Tsushima were classified into thirty ranks. These envoys exchanged *Sŏgye* with the Second (參判) or Third Minister (參議) of the Board of Rites (禮曹), in accordance with their ranks, and their respective formalities were also prescribed. The ranks, titles, and names of addressers and addressees, as well as forms of description in the *Sŏgye* were meticulously regulated.[4] Sovereigns' messages were also defined according to strict formalities.[5]

In this regard, it is necessary to mention a few words about *taetu* (c; *taitou*, 擡頭) which became a grave issue between the two countries after the Meiji Restoration. *Taetu* is a special form of writing in the Confucian world. It consists of the elevation of one letter in writing in order to express deference to a superior. There were three kinds of *taetu*. If a certain word related to the actions of the court, government, king or emperor, that word had to be written one space above the margin. Such a form of writing was called *tantae* (單擡). If it related to the character or actions of an emperor or empress, it had to be elevated two spaces above the margin. This was called *sangtae* (雙擡). Lastly. if it was concerned with the emperors' ancestors, three spaces had to be reserved above the margin, a form of *taetu* named *samtae* (三擡). This form of writing was strictly observed especially after the beginning of the Qing Dynasty in 1644 (清朝) (See figure 2. p. xiii).

The *Tosŏ*, a seal made of copper, was a trade certificate conferred by the Korean court to Japanese traders. The names of the relevant Japanese traders were engraved on a *Tosŏ* made by the Korean government. Since the Chief Lords of Tsushima monopolized Korean trade, their names were the only ones to appear on *Tosŏ* made thereafter. Such a *Tosŏ* system was similar to that of tally trade between the Ming (明) government and Japan.

---

4) CCKJ, Book 5; TMHG, vol., 4, pp. 3881 ff.

5) CCKJ, Book 5.

When a new seal was produced and conferred upon the Chief Lord of Tsushima, it was also stamped on papers which were kept in the Board of Rites in Seoul, and in the Magistracy at Pusan. Whenever Tsushima dispatched her *Sŏgye* stamped with the *Tosŏ*, Korean officials verified its authenticity with the papers which they kept. The oldest known *Tosŏ* was cast in 1418, and the last one was that conferred to So Yoshiaki (宗義達, 1847~1902, Chief Lord; 1863~1871) (See figure 3. p. xiv).

The Japan House

The Japan House (倭館) was similar, in a sense, to a Trading Factory (海外商館) established by Westerners in China. From 1757 to the outbreak of the Opium War (1839~1842), trade between China and Western countries was only permitted in one place, namely Guangzhou (廣州), and, even there, only during the trading season, from October to the following January. At this time, the place where foreigners were permitted to reside was called a 'factory.' It is needless to say that the Japan House in Korea was different from the Trading Factory in China in many respects, but the latter is cited here only as an analogy.

Japanese merchants were permitted to reside in particular places in Korea from the beginning of the fifteenth century. But from the seventeenth century until the Meiji Restoration in 1868, they resided in the Japan House in Ch'oryang (草梁), which was built in 1675~1678. Located around Mt. Yongdu (龍頭山), in Kwangbok

Tong (光復洞), in Pusan, it was 330,000 square meters in size (See figure 1. p. xii).

The population of Japanese permanent residents amounted to some 400 or 500 people, while Korean officials, including resident Koreans connected with the Japan House, numbered more than 3,000 men. It could easily be surmised that the Japan House occupied a very important place in Korean-Japanese relations. Thereby, the regulations concerning the Japan House were stipulated in great detail. Nevertheless, the new Japanese government following the Meiji Reformation tried to change the age-old *Kyorin* system, and thereupon began the unhappy period of the modern Korean-Japanese relationships.

1

The Clash between Two International Orders

__ Differences of Perception and Diplomatic Frictions

__ Problems Involving Korean Historical Sources

__ Revision of the Basic Framework of Korean-Japanese Relations

__ Korean Countermeasures

__ A Change in the Negotiating Partners: Officials of the Tsushima *fan* and of the Foreign Affairs Ministry

__ The Break-Out from the Japan House

Within the Kyorin *system, the* Sŏgye *was a specific kind of diplomatic document that called for the observance of a well-defined protocol.*[1] *Accordingly, altering the* Sŏgye *was not a simple formality. Rather, any change to its form raised the extremely pressing issue of how to interpret the norms of the then-existing international society.*

The late 1860s mark the unhappy beginning of modern Korean-Japanese relations. On the one hand, Japan was trying to unilaterally repudiate the norms of international society, while Korea, on the other hand, failed to grasp the historical circumstances, which rendered the norms of the Kyorin *relationship no longer applicable. This period illustrates the clash between two worldviews: one based on the* Kyorin *order, and the other founded on Western international law. Therefore, knowledge of the historical background is essential if we are to understand*

---

1) For the formality of the *Sŏgye*, see TMKJ, vol., 1, book 6; CCKJ, book 5; Yi Hun (1993).

how both countries were ultimately responsible for the historical conflicts that were to ensue.

Differences of Perception and Diplomatic Frictions

England and Japan were the first countries to destroy the *Sadae* and *Kyorin* orders of the Confucian world. By a strange coincidence, these two countries later became allies and played an important role in Far Eastern politics.

The breakdown of the *Sadae* order in the Chinese world began during the Opium War (1839~1842), while the decline of the *Kyorin* order originated with the internal political reformation in Japan, known as the Meiji Reformation (明治維新).

The dissolution of the *Kyorin* order was a consequence of its conflict with the system of Western international law. Such friction which spanned the period from the Meiji Restoration, on December 9, 1868, to the signing of the Treaty of Amity and Commerce between Korea and Japan, on February 2, 1876 did not end there. The mindset underlying those clashes resonates in the hearts of the people of both countries to the present day.

The origin of the breakdown of relations between the two countries in the years 1868~1876 resulted from their conflicting worldviews. For its part, the Korean government would not abandon the centuries-old policy of treating Japan as a partner in the *Kyorin* order. The new Japanese Meiji government, by contrast, denied the traditional intermediary role of Tsushima in Korean-Japanese relations and unified diplomatic affairs under its Ministry of Foreign Affairs. At the same time, Japan adopted a new policy of ascribing Korea inferior status, transforming the typical Japanese 'mental structure' of the period into actual diplomatic policy.

Furthermore, it should be remembered that the old tradition of mistrust and contempt between the two countries strongly contributed to this clash of worldviews. Therefore, it was not an easy task to maintain normal relations.

This period is too confusing and complicated to be clarified in a few paragraphs. In general, scholars explain the relationship between the two countries according to their own periodizations. I divide the eight-year conflict into three periods as follows:

(1) 1868~1870: from the time of the Japanese submission of a new *Sŏgye* to the Korean court to the Japanese Foreign Ministry's takeover of the Korean question;
(2) 1870~1873: from the time of the arrival of Japanese foreign ministry officials in Korea until the retirement of the Taewŏngun (大院君), the Regent;
(3) 1873~1876: from the beginning of the Korean King Kojong's (高宗) actual reign to the conclusion of the Kanghwa Treaty (江華島條約).

Problems Involving Korean Historical Sources

First of all, it should be noted that basic Korean sources, such as

SJWIG, ISN, and KJSL, do not fully record historical events during the years 1868~1871 when the two orders first encountered each other. In these sources, the first record on the matter of the *Sŏgye* is dated January 14, 1870. That record reads:

> The State Council (議政府) said as follows: according to the report of Chŏng Hyŏndŏk (鄭顯德), the prefect of Tongrae Prefecture (東萊府), there exist some problems to be ascertained referring to precedents, in the *Sŏgye* of Hira Yoshiaki (平義達), who was the chief of Tsushima *fan*, and in the letters of his new official title. The letters of the [Korean] language official (訓導) and of the assistant language official (別差) also indicate these problems. Chŏng said that in particular the insertion of imperial subject (朝臣) after the name of Hira was contrary to the established rule and that he ordered the [Korean] translators to admonish the Japanese to rectify the *Sŏgye* and to present a correct one.
>
> The State Council presented its decision: the new official title was contrary to the established rule and practice. How could this have happened considering the 300-years-old agreement? We must insist that the Japanese rectify the *Sŏgye*. We humbly ask for your orders. The King grants sanction.[2]

This record did not mention such important questions as the usage of the title 'Emperor' (皇), the term 'imperial edict' (勅), or the minting of a new Japanese seal. Tabohashi interpreted this Korean record as follows: the Korean court would have accepted the Japanese document if Japan had changed the name of the official title in the altered *Sŏgye* to Korea. As for the other matters,

---

2) SJWIG, 3, p. 386; ISN, 68, p. 230; KJSL, 1, p. 327.

it would have decided that the Board of Rites (禮曹) should protest against Japan's actions.

Tabohashi also made some conjectures as to the reasons for the paucity of Korean historical sources about Korean-Japanese negotiations during the years 1868~1871: the Korean court ordered the Board of Rites to examine the precedents and it decided to accept a new Japanese *Sŏgye*, as long as Japan agreed to Korea's demand. But the powerful entourage of the Taewŏngun; Kim Saeho (金世鎬), the governor of Kyŏngsang Province (慶尙道), Chŏng Hyŏndŏk, the Prefect of Tongrae, and An Tongjun (安東晙), the language official, had already concluded that they would not accept a new *Sŏgye*, regardless of whether Japan changed its contents. Consequently, Korean historical sources were silent regarding An Tongjun's negotiations with Japan.[3]

Tabohashi's hypothesis imputes all responsibility to the Taewŏngun and his entourage alone. However, attachment to this kind of interpretation inevitably results in the concealment of the underlying Japanese political motive for changing, by force, the norms of an existing international society. In this regard, Korean records for this period must be studied and explored further.

---

3) Tabohashi (1940), 1, pp. 180-182.

Revision of the Basic Framework of Korean-Japanese Relations

On September 7, 1868, the Meiji government appointed Kawamoto Kusaemon (川本九左衛門) as a special official in order to inform the Korean court of the Meiji Reformation in Japan. Thus, began the preliminary negotiations of the *Sŏgye*. Before delving more deeply into the details of these negotiations, let us first briefly examine the Japanese policy prior to the appointment of Kawamoto as envoy to Korea.

In Osaka(大阪), three important meetings were held at Gaikokukan (外國官)[4] on May 12, 14 and 17, 1868. Komatsu Tatewaki (小松帶刀) and Nakai Koso (中井弘藏), high officials of the Gaikokukan, held these conferences together with Oshima Tomonoso (大島友之允), a high-ranking official of the Tsushima *fan* stationed in Kyoto.[5] These meetings resulted in important

---

4) Gaikokukan (外國官, June 1868~August 1869), a predecessor of the present Ministry of Foreign Affairs (外務省), continued in existence first in Osaka, Kyoto, and later in Tokyo.

5) Guarding the traditional relationship with Korea was a matter of life or death to the Tsushima *fan*. When the problem of establishing a new pattern of international relations between Japan and Korea arose after the Meiji Reformation, relations between the Meiji Govenment and the Tsushima *fan* understandably became strained. The Meiji Government decided to maintain the status quo as far as the Tsushima's role was concerned, but asked the Tsushima *fan* to notify Korea of the Meiji Reformation in the orders of March 23 and April 22, 1868. Accordingly, So Yoshiaki of the Tsushima *fan*, submitted a long report to Gaikokukan.

decisions, which directly contributed to the ensuing tensions between the two countries, a rift that would last for the following eight years. Their decisions were as follows:

(1) The names of the five imperial predecessors, including the present Meiji emperor, will no longer be used;

(2) The Korean government should be informed of the inauguration of the new Meiji government;

(3) The use of the seals endowed by the Korean court, and traditionally used by Tsushima in the conduct of Korean affairs, is of a dubious nature considering the new Japanese national politic. Therefore, new seals will be minted by the Japanese government;

(4) The forms of address in the sovereigns' letters should be changed. 'Emperor' should be used for the Japanese King. Consequently the status of the Korean King would be lowered;

(5) As a means of carrying out diplomatic reform, it is necessary to elevate Tsushima's own status and to strengthen his position. The rank enjoyed by So Yoshiaki (宗義達) should also be raised

---

In this report, So Yoshiaki provided an account of diplomatic relations between Korea and Japan, and the inevitable importance of Korean trade to Tsushima. He also outlined some drawbacks concerning existing trade relations, and concluded that if Korea did not accept the Japanese proposal, Japan would be forced to retaliate. Gaikokukan was at a loss as to how to handle the Korean question. As a temporary remedy, Gaikokukan ordered So Yoshiaki to consult Date Munenari (伊達宗城), Vice-Minister of the Gaikokukan and Komats, a high official of the same organization. Such was the backdrop for the conferences which took place during the month of May. Tabohashi (1940), 1, pp. 137-143; Arano (1988), pp. 252-253; So's memorial can be found in NGB, 1/1, doc. no. 288, pp. 657-671.

accordingly.[6]

Needless to say, these decisions threatened to destroy the norms of international society as it then stood. In particular, the use of the term 'Emperor' for the Japanese king which was designed to degrade the status of his Korean counterpart, along with the discontinuation of the use of traditional seals, amounted to a concealed design of total modification to Korean-Japanese relations.[7] Thus, Kawamoto was sent to Korea and the important points of the *Sŏgye* that he brought could be paraphrased as follows:

(1) The phraseology of the chief's name of the Tsushima *fan* was changed;

(2) In regard to the Japanese king, the *Sŏgye* used terminologies like 'Emperor' and 'Edicts'. But under the *Sadae* international order these words were only for the Chinese emperor and its court. As already mentioned, Japan used these words in order to assign a distinctly inferior status to Korea;

---

6) Tabohashi (1940), 1, pp. 144-145.

7) The Meiji government did not encounter any obstacles in concluding the Treaty of Amity and Trade with China. Since the advent of the Qing Dynasty, there had been no official diplomatic relations between the two governments. The only contact between China and Japan occurred through merchants stationed at Nagasaki. In this sense, they had only private relations. But Korean-Japanese relations were of an essentially different nature. Korea and Japan had shared institutions and practices for several hundred years. They therefore lived within a more closely-knit international society, a longstanding arrangement that Japan now intended to radically alter.

(3) From now on, the Japanese government would dispatch a 'special envoy' to negotiate the normalization of Japanese-Korean relations and a new seal would be stamped in his letter of credential.

(4) The reason for the use of a new seal was especially peculiar as shown in the excerpt below:

> The special envoy's letter was stamped with a new seal which represents the sincerity of our court, and your country ought to accept it. The reason for receiving seals from your country since ancient times was a favor of a private nature. But all of this [i.e. the change of seals: author] being related to the special orders of our court, how can the public (公) be damaged by the private (私)?[8]

This explanation was of great implicit significance because the centuries-old relationship between Korea and Tsushima was defined as 'private', while that of Korea and the Meiji government was labeled 'public'. The special envoy, Higuchi Tetsushiro (樋口鐵四郎), came to Korea with this important mission at the end of 1868. Due to Korea's refusal to meet the special envoy, however, he was unable to achieve any results.

Korean Countermeasures

As soon as Kawamoto and his party arrived at the Japan House in Ch'oryang (草梁), the language official, An Tongjun, and his assistant, Yi Chuhyŏn met with them on December 12. These

---

8) YHHN, 4, pp. 211-212; NGB, 1/2, doc. no. 705, p. 691; ZRSM, Book 1.

Korean officials vociferously protested against both the contents of the Japanese *Sŏgye* and the sending of a special envoy to the Korean court as acts contrary to the established regulations. They flatly rejected the Japanese proposal:

> We have no intention of receiving the *Sŏgye* at all, and even if the special envoy came to Korea, the Korean court would never receive such a person, as such an appointment is contrary to the regulations. The Japanese should cease to raise this troublesome issue in the future.[9]

An Tongjun proposed postponing the meeting until January of the next year, and both parties agreed.

On February 29, 1869, An Tongjun visited Urase Hiroshi (浦瀬 裕), the Japanese translator and handed over an official document which he had received from the Korean government the day before.[10] The following is a summary of its main points:

(1) Korea and Japan had been keeping faith with each other for three hundred years and had established the Japan House in Korea for negotiations. This could be defined as a grand law (大 經, 大法).

(2) The changing of the official title of the chief of the Tsushima *fan* and the words 'imperial subject' (朝臣), used in the *Sŏgye*, were contrary to the regulations.

(3) The phrase "the public is damaged by the private" in the *Sŏgye* and the minting of a new seal could not be accepted at any cost.

---

9) YHHN, 4, pp. 214-215.
10) NGB, 2-2, enclosure of doc. no. 320, pp. 227-228; ZRSM, Book 1.

Thus, the first official encounter between Korea and the Meiji government resulted in rupture.

On November 9, 1869, Korea presented a concrete and detailed statement refuting Japanese proposals. An Tongjun gave two important memoranda to the Japanese delegation which warrant closer examination. In the memorandum signed by himself, he condemned Japan's actions; the two countries had been on good diplomatic terms for such a long time. For 300 years, no such document as the new Japanese *Sŏgye* in question had ever been proposed.[11]

The other memorandum, signed by both An and Yi, consists of a point-by-point rebuttal of Japanese assertions.[12]

(1) The change of the chief's title of the Tsushima *fan*: his position should be changed to a higher one according to his merits, and his new rank could be used in Japan, but in the *Koryin* documents, there is a regulation about formalities and this regulation cannot be altered in any way without prior consultation with the Korean government.

(2) The use of the term 'imperial subject' before the name of the *fan*'s chief: even though he is a high official, it is contrary to the regulations to write his official title between his family name and given name.

(3) The stamping of a new seal in *Sŏgye*: Tsushima should use the seals issued by the Korean court. This signifies the fidelity between both parties. Therefore, the seal is not to be changed.

(4) The use of a new honorific title for the Korean Second Minister

11) NGB, 2/3, doc. no. 616, pp. 413-414; ZRSM, Book 1.
12) NGB, 2/3, doc. no. 615, pp. 410-412; ZRSM, Book 1.

(參判) of the Board of Rites: *Taein* (大人) perhaps has the same meaning as *Kong* (公), but for three hundred years, *Taein* has been used and the sudden use of *Kong* cannot be accepted.

(5) The use of 'Imperial House (皇室)': the use of the word 'Emperor' can be applied only to those who have conquered the world. Therefore, although that title could perhaps be used in Japan, it is not to be written in the *Sŏgye*.

(6) The use of 'Edict (勅)': 'Edict' means an Emperor's order. It should not even be necessary to say that the word could never be written in documents of the *Koryin* order.

(7) The use of the word 'private': Tsushima received seals from Korea out of Korean favor, not out of Korean private relations with Tsushima. The receiving of seals should not be attributed to private feelings. The phrase "The private damages the public" is really objectionable.

(8) The composition of diplomatic documents is strictly regulated: the agreements of the two countries ought not to be changed arbitrarily. The *Sŏgye* is not a document in which rough and unpolished words should be used. Even if only one word ignores the regulations, it cannot be accepted. In Japan, there must be those who know the rules. It is most regrettable that things have turned out this way.

The Japanese refuted the Korean position in the form of an oral statement[13] as follows:

(1) The names of official ranks can apply to relations between neighboring countries. There exists a fixed form in the *Sŏgye*, but the location and style of characters can be changed. The conduct

---

13) NGB, 2/3, doc. no. 617, pp. 414-418.

of affairs requires constancy as well as expediency.

(2) The term 'imperial subject' was used in the past, and the reason for the sudden refusal to use the word is incomprehensible.

(3) The new seal was inevitable because of the changes in the Japanese system of government.

(4) The unified usage of the terms *Kong* or *Taein* would raise some questions in the writing style. From now on, *Kakno* (閣老) will be used and it will be made equal in both countries.

(5) Japan has become an imperial state now. Therefore it is appropriate to use 'Emperor' or 'Edict'. Mr. Urase, our translator, has explained the word 'private' to you and it will not be necessary to discuss it again.

The Korean logic was very much in keeping with the viewpoint of the *Kyorin* order. To change the formalities of the diplomatic documents requires prior agreement between all international parties. This holds true for any form of international society. While the Korean stance was based on the logic of the existing international society at that time, the Japanese position was to negate that form of international society, by insisting on the use of another logic based on the order of Western international law. Thus, the two countries failed to reach an agreement, due to the conflicting political founding principles of the two orders.

A Change in the Negotiating Partners: Officials of the Tsushima *fan* and of the Foreign Affairs Ministry

The Meiji government blamed Tsushima's influence on Korean

affairs as the main reason for the impasse between the two countries. It finally decided that the traditional role of Tsushima would be abolished. Japanese Foreign Affairs officials presented a document entitled 'An Investigative Document on Korea'[14] to Dajokan (太政官, the Council of State).

This document illustrates the atmosphere of Japanese political circles of the time very succinctly. A summary of the important parts is as follows:

(1) For almost two hundred years, Japan gave Tsushima a mandate to maintain diplomatic relations with Korea and Tsushima-Korean negotiations have been based on 'private' relations. The mandate of the Tsushima *fan* for Korean affairs should come to an end.

(2) If foreign powers inquired about this matter according to Western international law, the Japanese government could not explain it.

(3) In the past, Japan had once occupied Korea. Therefore, only Japan could now prevent other powers, including Russia, from invading Korea.

This document represents precisely the Japanese attitude that only Japan could prevent Korea from becoming a colony of other countries and that Korea was the 'life line (生命線)' to Japan.[15] Furthermore, Japan made it clear in this document that it intended to dissolve the *Kyorin* order and to establish in its place another

---

14) NGB, 2/2, doc. no. 488, pp. 855-857.
15) Arano (1988), p. 264.

order, one based on Western international law.

Tsushima strongly resisted such a decision made by the Ministry of Foreign Affairs. The change of officials in charge of the negotiations created problems for Japan's internal policies. Therefore, the Meiji government was compelled to take several initial steps before the Foreign Ministry officials could participate as negotiating partners with Korea. First, the Japanese government decided to concede to Tsushima's demands and, for the time being, took steps toward sending government officials to Korea as investigators. The next step was for Japanese government officials to go to Pusan, not as investigators, but as full negotiating partners, even though the Tsushima officials were still in charge of actual negotiations. Finally, after this process, the officials of the Meiji government moved to the forefront, taking over the Japan House from the Tsushima's officials.

Sata Hakubo (佐田白茅) and Moriyama Shigeru (森山茂), the investigators of the Foreign Ministry, who disguised themselves as Tsushima officials, stayed at the Japan House for about one month in February 1870. Both men reported back to the Japanese government in a secret investigation of the Korean problem and recommended the use of force, if necessary.[16]

The Foreign Ministry reported to the Council of State that they had to choose one of three directions concerning a policy towards Korea:[17]

---

16) NGB, 3, doc. nos. 87, 88, pp. 131-143.
17) NGB, 3, doc. no. 89, pp. 144-145, n. d..

(1) Japan would break off diplomatic relations with Korea assuming the attitude of an onlooker in the event of a Russian invasion of Korea.

(2) Japan would send Kido Takayoshi (木戸孝允) to Korea as a diplomatic delegate with two warships and if the necessary occasion arose, Japan would use force.

(3) Since Korea was a semi-tributary country of China, Japan should take steps to make a treaty with China, in order to place Korea in an inferior position and later condemn any interference from China if a conflict arose between Korea and Japan.

The Japanese government decided to adopt the third policy and send Yanagihara Sakimitsu (柳原前光) to China in July 1870 in order to conclude a treaty.

While the conflict between the Tsushima *fan* and the Ministry of Foreign Affairs over negotiation partners with Korea continued, the Japanese government sent Foreign Ministry officials, Yoshioka Koki (吉岡弘毅), Moriyama Shigeru, and Hirotsu Hironobu (廣津弘信) to Pusan on November 3, 1870. Although they failed to conclude a treaty with the Korean government, they stayed in Pusan for a year.[18]

Meanwhile, the repeal of the role of the Tsushima *fan* continued to be a controversial issue in Japan. The Japanese government succeeded in introducing a modern system of administration (廢藩置縣, abolition of domains) by July 1871, when the Japanese Foreign Affairs office assumed direct control over matters concerning Korea. Nevertheless, in view of the fact that Tsushima had been Korea's negotiating partner for several hundred years,

---

18) Sim Jaegi (1997), pp. 67-200; Min Dŏkgi (1994), pp. 19-47.

the Japanese government appointed the chief of the Tsushima *fan*, So Yoshiaki (宗義達), as a high official in the Ministry of Foreign Affairs. Likewise Sagara Masaki (相良正樹), So's former subject, was appointed to an official post in the same organization, in order to aid in the negotiations with the Korean government.

The Break-Out from Japan House

The Korean government could not perceive the secret motives behind the sudden change of negotiators by their Japanese counterpart. Accordingly, Korea insisted on negotiating only with the officials of the Tsushima *fan* as had been the custom in the past. To accomplish this, Korea sent two strong dispatches to the Chief Lord of Tsushima, So Yoshiaki, which were written by Chŏng Hyŏndŏk (鄭顯德), the Prefect of Tongrae, and Kim Ch'ŏlgyun (金徹均), the Army Commander (僉使) in Pusan, in September 1871 (by the lunar calendar).[19] These dispatches strongly refuted the Japanese decision to appoint the officials of the Foreign Ministry as negotiating partners with Korea.

Meanwhile, Sagara Masaki dared to rush out from the restricted area of the Japan House and demanded to meet the Prefect of Tongrae face to face. Sagara's unexpected behavior, of course, was infeasible without prior consultation with Yoshioka, Moriyama, and Hirotsu, the Japanese Foreign Ministry officials. As already

19) NGB, 4, doc. no. 211, pp. 329-330.

explained in the Introduction, leaving the boundaries of the Japan House without official Korean permission was an illegal act and a breach of the regulations of the *Kyorin* order. This incident obviously represented the Japanese intention to radically change the longstanding political framework between the two countries.

With this incident as a momentum, in August 1872, the Japanese Foreign Ministry ordered Hanabusa Yoshimoto (花房義質) to take over the Japan House and sent Moriyama Shigeru and Okugi Isamu (奥義制) to serve on duty in Korea. Sagara was sent back to Tsushima and Hukami Masakage (深見正景), the Chief of the Japan House, was dismissed. Finally, the Japan House was under the complete control of Foreign Ministry officials.

As a direct consequence of these events, the negotiations between the two countries came to a deadlock and there also arose in Japan a strong movement of *Seikanron* (征韓論, arguments over whether to conquer Korea). As we saw in the Introduction, however, such a Japanese attitude toward Korea was not a new phenomenon, but a tradition of long standing. It is therefore meaningless to seek the exact date of the beginning of *Seikanron* movement, or to connect such movement with the *Sŏgye*.

The first and second period of the relationship between the two countries ended when the Japanese Foreign Ministry took over the Japan House. The third period commenced when epoch-making political changes occurred in Korea. The Korean government finally understood the underlying Japanese political motive and adopted a policy to actively cope with the new international situation. Such a new Korean policy shall be further examined in the following chapter.

2

Korea's New Japanese Policy

__ Controversy between the Taewŏngun and Pak Kyusu over Diplomatic
   Policy
__ The Change in Korean Policy toward Japan
__ The Korean Board of Rites and the Japanese Ministry of Foreign
   Affairs
__ The Lonely Struggle of King Kojong (1)
__ The Lonely Struggle of King Kojong (2)

The Taewŏngun (大院君), the Regent, who had refused for almost ten years to negotiate with Japan and the Western powers, finally receded from the actual political scene in 1873. In the 1860s, the Taewŏngun had been able to refuse to engage with the external world owing to the then-international circumstances.

England, the leading world power, endeavored to maintain her cooperative policy with China after attaining the political and economic springboard to encroach upon the Chinese market. Having achieved this, England did not want to confront China on the question of the Korean peninsula.

Russia, another leading world power, was, likewise, compelled to pursue 'a waiting policy' regarding the Korean problem owing to her economic underdevelopment. Consequently, Russia wanted to maintain a status quo in the Korean peninsula as well.

Japan, the potential disturber of the Sadae order, could not put any definite Korean policy into effect before 1871 owing to her own internal political disunity. In 1871 Japan finally succeeded to accomplish the abolition of domains (廢藩置縣) and the Japanese Ministry of Foreign Affairs began to take direct control over the Korean question.

From the advent of the 1870s, the international political conditions surrounding Korea drastically differed from those of the earlier decade. Kojong, the eminent Korean King, and Pak Kyusu, the father of the Enlightenment Movement in Korea, perceived the historical inevitability of Korea's encounter with the outside world.

Controversy between the Taewŏngun and Pak Kyusu over Diplomatic Policy

A new diplomatic policy was adopted when the Taewŏngun resigned from his political position on December 12 (lunar Nov. 3), 1873, and King Kojong henceforth directly governed the state.

Japan watched carefully as events unfolded in the Korean court. On March 14, 1874, Okugi Isamu (奧義制), who was working at the Japan House, sent Moriyama Shigeru (森山茂), in Japan, the following news: the retirement of the Regent and his followers, King Kojong's assumption of actual control over the government, and the imminent dismissal of the prefect of Tongrae Prefecture (東萊府使).[1]

In response, Prime Minister Sanjo Sanetomi (三條實美) ordered

---

1) NGB, 7, doc. no. 206, pp. 349-350.

Moriyama, on May 15, 1874, to return to Korea in order to directly investigate the internal affairs of the Korean court. By June 21, Moriyama sent an important report to Japan entitled 'Recent Situation in Korea.' Its contents are as follows:

(1) The rumor about the power struggle in the Korean court has prevailed since last winter. The Regent retired from the actual political world and King Kojong is governing in person now.
(2) Chŏng Hyŏndŏk and An Tongjun will soon be dismissed.
(3) The Korean court is well aware of the *Seikanron* movement in Japan and has been carefully observing Japan.[2]

There remain in related research works some untenable assumptions or hypotheses as regards this epoch-making political event in Korea. For instance, the assumption that the Regent's political influence over conservative circles disappeared after his retirement, or the hypothesis that King Kojong's active policy toward Japan borrowed from the laidback way of thinking of Queen Min's family, are hardly credible. Further, it is far from a historical fact that Korea had only to surrender in the face of the pressure of Japan's gunboat diplomacy.

Nevertheless the establishment of normal relations with Japan was still the first and foremost concern of the Korean court, even after the Regent receded into the background. On the question of normalization with Japan, the Korean court was divided into supporters and dissenters, and the theoretical confrontation of

---

2) NGB, 7, doc. no, 210, pp. 364-366.

these two groups could be found in the arguments between the Taewŏngun and Pak Kyusu (朴珪壽).

It can be said, generally speaking, that conservative forces exerted overwhelming influence in the court at that time. King Kojong was therefore forced to undergo a lonely struggle against these powerful conservatives, whom his biological father, the Taewŏngun, still supported. On the other hand, Pak Kyusu was the very person who counseled King Kojong on the necessity of a new foreign policy. During the *General Sherman* incident in 1866, when he was the Governor of Pyongan Province (平安道), Pak even upheld the necessity of making contact with the United States.[3] Upon being appointed Minister of the Board of Punishments (刑曹判書) and Chief Magistrate of Seoul Magistracy (漢城府尹), he came to Seoul in July 1869. From that time until his death in 1877, his actions should be considered of great importance for the development of modern Korean history.

After the retirement of the Regent, Pak must have strongly appealed to King Kojong to accept a new Japanese *Sŏgye*. The Taewŏngun was the first to send a letter to Pak, in which he claimed that Korea should not accept the *Sŏgye*.[4]

Thus commenced the argument between these two people. To put it in modern terms, it was an argument about the basic direction of Korean diplomatic policy. However, since only Pak's letters to the Taewŏngun are extant today in the *Pak Kyusu Chŏnjip* (朴珪壽全集, the Complete Works of Pak Kyusu), there are

---

3) For his idea of international politics, see Yongkoo Kim (2001), pp. 82-91.
4) YHHN, 4, pp. 326-329.

some limitations in attempting to reconstruct the arguments.

Since Pak's first letter to the Taewŏngun in 1874 seems to be very important, I will attempt to explain that letter in detail, while quoting related phrases from other letters.[5] Even though Pak was serving as the Governor of Pyongan Province, far from Seoul, he came to know about the *Sŏgye* problem, due to the assistance of Pang Usŏ (方禹叙), a translator, who wrote to him in detail about the issue. Pak summarized his own dissenting opinions against the Korean court's rejection of the Japanese *Sŏgye* as follows:

(1) The Title Change of Tsushima's Chief Lord: the intention of the Japanese government was to exaggerate the fact that they had newly established their own political system. Therefore it was beyond our concern and the change should be considered to be an internal matter of a neighboring country.

(2) The Use of 'Emperor' or 'Edict': Japanese people had addressed their king as an 'Emperor' for the last thousand years. They are entitled to do so in order to display their respect toward their own king. There exists the historical precedent that during the reign of King Kojong (高宗) of the Ting (唐) Dynasty, China once received a dispatch from Japan, which referred to the Japanese king as 'the Son of Heaven (天子).'

---

5) Pak's letters in PKSCJ, 1, are as follows:
(1) Pak's letters sent to the Taewŏngun; [a] pp. 749-754, written in 1874. [b] pp. 754-757, written in Jan. (lunar), 1875, [c] pp. 757-760, written in May (lunar), 1875, [d] pp. 760-762, n. d., [e] pp. 763-768, n. d.
(2) Pak's letters sent to Yi Ch'oeŭng (李最應); [a] pp. 768-769, written in Feb. (lunar), 1875, [b] pp. 769-770, n. d., [c] pp. 770-771, n. d., [d] 771-775, n. d., [e] pp. 775-776, n. d., [f] p. 777, n. d., [g] 777-778, n. d., [h] 778-779, n. d., [i] pp. 779-781, n. d.

(3) The Elevation of One Letter above the Margin (to express deference to royalty) when writing the Japanese Imperial Household (皇室): the Japanese *Sŏgye* elevates one letter in writing 'Imperial House', but does not elevate letters in writing 'Korean Country.' 'Japanese Country,' 'Your Country,' 'This Country', to show deference. The *Sŏgye* does not mention our King as the Most Revered (至尊). If it did, it might have elevated one letter above the margin.[6]

(4) The Discontinuance of Usage of *Tosŏ* conferred by Korea: the use of *Tosŏ* is, in essence, redundant and needless. Are we asking Japan to be our vassal?

Therefore Pak concluded as follows: even in personal relations, one bears a grudge if one does not receive answers to one's letters. Japan must have felt increasing anger toward us because we have refused the Japanese *Sŏgye* for several years. Since Japan and the Western powers are one, it would be foolish to make one more enemy.[7]

The great disagreement between the Taewŏngun and Pak, in fact, represented the atmosphere in the Korean court in those years. In the meantime, Korea's new Japanese policy was formulated by King Kojong and his entourage.

---

6) See also Pak's letter (1)-[d].

7) Pak's letter (1)-[e] also analyzed the *Sŏgye* problem in detail.

The Change in Korean Policy toward Japan

On August 11 (Lunar June 29), 1874, a very important court meeting was held. At this meeting, Yi Yuwŏn (李裕元), the Chief State Councilor (領議政), raised an issue which he deemed of the utmost urgency and importance. Yi demanded the punishment of An Tongjun, the language officer who was the Regent's devotee, on the grounds that An had mismanaged relations between Korea and Japan.

Subsequently, Pak Kyusu, the Third State Councilor (右議政), expressed almost the same idea as Yi. Pak added further that Japan referred to their king as 'Emperor' in order to respect their own king and that they had never asked Korea to designate him in the same way. Pak also stated that there was nothing strange about Japan's decision to change the title of the Tsushima's Chief Lord, and that Korea's rejection of the *Sŏgye* for these reasons was therefore against the rule of the *Kyorin* relationship.[8] Finally, Yi and Pak requested permission to send interpreters to Japan in order to closely investigate Japanese internal politics. On August 14, the Korean court informed the Japan House of its intention to send interpreters to Japan. Thus, the relationships between the two countries entered a new phase.

Korea came to have an official meeting with Moriyama, an official of the Japanese Ministry of Foreign Affairs. But before that

---

8) SJIG, 4, pp. 881-882; ISN, 70, p. 301; KJSL, 1, p. 466.

official conference, the Korean government utilized an informal route in order to determine the actual intentions of the Japanese. To this end, on August 28, three members among the secret royal inspectors who went to Pusan for the investigation of An Tongjun's blunder had a long meeting with Moriyama. These three people blamed An, as well as Chŏng Hyŏndŏk for recent events, and they made it clear that Korea was determined to take serious steps to deal with Japan in the future.[9] It is needless to say that such secret contact was only possible with the permission of King Kojong.

The Korean Board of Rites and the Japanese Ministry of Foreign Affairs

Hyŏn Sŏkun (玄昔運), a new language officer, had a meeting with Moriyama in early September 1874.[10] This was the first time that a Korean representative met a Japanese Foreign Ministry official. At this meeting, they agreed to conduct negotiations in the future concerning one of the three following agendas:

(1) Would the Japanese *Sŏgye* of 1872 be accepted by the Korean court?

(2) If that *Sŏgye* was unacceptable, would a new *Sŏgye* be produced

---

9) NGB, 7, enclosure in doc. no. 214, pp. 387-395.
10) NGB, 7, enclosure 3 in doc. no. 215, pp. 398-400. The exact date of this meeting is not clear.

in Japan again and sent to the Korean Board of Rites?

(3) If the two agendas above were unacceptable, would the Korean court compose a new draft and dispatch an envoy to Tokyo?

The Korean court decided to take the second route. Thus, on September 19 (Lunar, August 9), Yi Yuwŏn presented a memorial to the Throne that Korea would restore the old amiable relationship with Japan if Japan submitted a correctly revised *Sŏgye*. King Kojong gave his sanction.[11]

On February 24, 1875, Moriyama returned to Pusan with a new *Sŏgye*. This new *Sŏgye* also raised another serious problem. The contents of it are as follows:

> We communicated to your government that our Emperor ruled the state in person, that the Ministry of Foreign Affairs was newly established and the title of the Tsushima's Chief Lord was changed. But Korea has refused to have an interview with a new Japanese envoy for seven years. This is not the right courtesy under the *Kyorin* order and is contrary to the old amiable harmony. Therefore, externally we were unable to uphold our Emperor's edicts and internally our whole nation was moved to great anger. This is a really regrettable outcome for your country. However, when Moriyama, our Ministry of Foreign Affairs official, met your officials last time, we discovered that some wily group had interfered with his superior's opinions, and that your court's resolutions were quite different. We wish that this group be punished. This is not to blame your government, but out of a desire for sincere relations between

---

11) KJSL, 1. p. 472. Hyŏn's letter sent to Moriyama can be found in NGB, 7, enclosure 3 of doc. no. 218, pp. 411-412; ZRSM, book 1.

our two countries. We wish that permanent justice be established by punishing that wily circle. We are sending back the three seals, which your country minted and sent to us.[12]

This new *Sŏgye* must have caused even more objections in Korea. The Korean court considered the phrase about the 'anger of the whole nation' as a threat, and they saw the Japanese demand that the 'wily group' be punished as an interference in domestic politics. Furthermore, the Japanese delegation neglected the age-old protocol of submitting the *Sŏgye* through the Japan House. They directly appeared before the magistrate's office of the Tongrae Prefecture.

Finally, a Korean language officer examined the new *Sŏgye* and found that the original copy was written in Japanese and stamped with the seal of the Japanese Ministry of the Foreign Affairs. Though the word 'the Son of Heaven' which had been used in the previous *Sŏgye* was omitted, words such as 'the Great Japan' and 'Emperor' were still used. Therefore, Korea decided not to accept the new *Sŏgye*.[13]

The Lonely Struggle of King Kojong (1)

Due to the new *Sŏgye* from Japan, the argument between the Taewŏngun and Pak Kyusu started again. Pak was opposed to the

---

12) NGB, 8, doc. no. 16, pp. 49-51; ZRSM, book 1.
13) YHHN, 4, pp. 323-326.

Taewŏngun's opinion of rejecting the new *Sŏgye*. They differed on the interpretation of the premise that 'Japan and the West are one (倭洋一體).' The Taewŏngun said that if Korea once accepts the *Sŏgye* and shows her weakness, they would invade Korea in concert. Pak retorted that because of their unity, Korea should not make either of them an enemy. Pak's logic continues as follows; Strength and weakness do not depend upon accepting the *Sŏgye* or not, but upon the management of affairs with reason and the conduct of human relations with civility.

The Taewŏngun quoted a classical saying that the word 'peace (和)' is the cause of putting the country in danger. But Pak retorted that he could not find its classical sources.[14]

On March 12 (Lunar, February 5), the Korean court, on the other hand, opened discussions on the new *Sŏgye* problem. The court had already received, from the Prefect of Tongrae, the dispatch dated February 19, in which he stated that he would not accept the new *Sŏgye*.

But King Kojong ordered, in the meeting of March 12, to accept the *Sŏgye* for the time being, because rejecting it for such a long time was not the right attitude from the *Kyorin* viewpoint. In addition, the new problems concerning the *Sŏgye* should be discussed with Japan again. Furthermore, King Kojong gave the opinion that the Prefect of Tongrae should go to the Japan House in order to discuss the pending problems. He went as far as to emphasize that even if Japanese envoys came to Korea aboard a

---

14) Pak's letter, (1)-[b]. Pak also reiterated his opinion to Yi Ch'oeŭng. See his letter (2)-[a].

steamship it was of no importance. Opposed to King Kojong's markedly positive attitude, Yi Ch'oeŭng (李最應), the second state councilor (左議政), and Kim Pyŏngguk (金炳國), the third state councilor (右議政), held him back. The discussion of that particular day was of such importance that we will examine it closely:

> King: What is the reason for the delay in responding to the dispatch of the Prefect of Tongrae?
>
> Ch'oeŭng: Since this issue is a very important matter relating to the *Kyorin*, we are going to reply after drawing the final conclusion through serious discussions with the full body of state councilors, including those who have retired from the post.
>
> King: It would not be sincere and trustworthy behavior, if we were to ignore the *Sŏgye* completely this time again.
>
> Ch'oeŭng: Your order is absolutely right, your Majesty.
>
> Pyŏngguk: Japanese people are so cunning that we cannot trust whatever they said on a previous day. This time the *Sŏgye* was written in Chinese mixed with the Korean letters, which had never been done before. It would be well-advised to examine the *Sŏgye* carefully in detail and if there should be anything against the regulations, we should reject it.

Afterwards, King Kojong said that Moriyama and his entourage should not be permitted to leave the boundaries of the Japan House and that the Tongrae Prefect should visit the Japan House for further discussion. Then, he continued to talk with Kim Pyŏngguk:

> King: It has been several days since the dispatch arrived from

Tongrae. It needs immediate action, because the current Japanese behavior betrays no sign of abating.

Pyŏngguk: The second state councilor's opinion addressed to the Throne that the *Sŏgye* question should be fully discussed with all the state councilors would be reasonable.

King: Are there any changes made in the new *Sŏgye*?

Pyŏngguk: Only the word 'the Son of Heaven' was deleted, but the words 'the Great' or 'Emperor' remained intact.

King: The Japanese envoys came to Korea aboard a steamship this time. It is because they have already established relations with the Western powers and there is no need to criticize them for that.

Pyŏngguk: Your order is absolutely right, your Majesty. But there is a precedent for visiting each other aboard a sailing boat. Coming aboard a Westernized ship doesn't seem strange and queer? This matter should be inquired into.[15]

King Kojong ordered the problem to be solved even in the middle of the night after consulting with the Tongrae prefect. The Council of State (議政府), under the kings' orders, reluctantly decided that the Tongrae Prefect should go to the Japan House and accept only the part of the *Sŏgye* that was written in Chinese.[16]

Notwithstanding the King's progressive attitudes, the conservative forces in the Council of State took advantage of the dispatch of Hwang Chŏngyŏn (黃正淵), the Prefect of Tongrae.

---

15) There are some differences in SJWIG, ISN, and KJSL. I reorganized the dialogue considering these materials. See SJWIG, 5, p. 130; ISN, 70, pp. 752-753; KJSL, 1, p. 492.

16) See the report of the Council of the State, KJSL, 1, p. 492.

Hwang had reported to the court that giving a special feast for his Japanese counterpart should be reconsidered. The Council of State addressed a memorial to the Throne that the *Sŏgye* question should be discussed anew.[17] This memorial was quite contrary to the decision that it had made immediately before.

While surrounded by a great number of conservatives, King Kojong and some of his followers were very anxious to resolve the Japanese matter. This entourage, who supported King Kojong, was later labeled the 'Progressive Party (開化派)' by historians, as will be discussed later in this book. Pak Kyusu was the head of this progressive movement and O Kyŏngsŏk (吳慶錫), Hyŏn Sŏkun (玄昔運) and Kang Wi (姜瑋) were his supporters. At that time, King Kojong was deeply in favor of this group.

The Lonely Struggle of King Kojong (2)

The Korean court held a very important meeting on June 13 (Lunar May 10), 1875, however, its decision resulted in a rupture between Korea and Japan. In spite of the tremendous efforts of King Kojong and Pak, the meeting finally concluded with the rejection of the new Japanese *Sŏgye*. The meeting that day was summoned by King Kojong and all the state councilors, as well as all the top officials with the rank above upper-senior third-grade (堂上官) were asked to attend the meeting.

---

17) KJSL, 1, p. 496.

The king himself queried all participants to express their own preferences. The majority of them strongly opposed accepting the new *Sŏgye*, while others asked for more prudence before accepting it, despite the fact that King Kojong and Pak insisted on normalizing relations between the two countries by accepting the new *Sŏgye*. The meeting continued until noon and since the weather was very hot, King Kojong suggested a change of venue for a cooler place, where the meeting continued. King Kojong urged the members to reach a swift and final decision about the matter through thorough discussion. To counter this urge, Yi Yuwŏn, the chief state councilor, and Kim Pyŏngguk retorted that the decision had been already made by the King and that further discussion was no longer needed, putting the King in a lonely and difficult position. The record of that meeting is of great importance and should be reviewed:

> King: I have to summon this conference urgently. No more time should be wasted because the *Sŏgye* is a matter concerning the political situation of the national boundaries. As to the *Sŏgye*, it is necessary to ask many opinions before sending a reply to Japan.
>
> Yuwŏn: It has been several years since this matter has been unresolved. The only pending problem is to accept or to reject the *Sŏgye*. But there is no unified opinion regarding this matter. To accept the *Sŏgye* is only a partial solution, which may breed innumerable problems. [He avoids the responsibility by saying further that he does not understand the problem well because of his stupidity.]
>
> Pyŏngguk: The reason why we refuse the *Sŏgye* is because of a few

words. During the Spring and Autumn period (春秋) in China, the kings of the O (吳) and Ch'o (楚) dynasties usurped the thrones, but they were considered kings in their own countries. However, when they dispatched their envoys to other countries, they described themselves as 'humble princes (寡君)' in order to show respect for other countries. In the Japanese *Sŏgye*, they addressed themselves with titles that were completely ridiculous and had never been mentioned before in any previous dispatches. That is why we still reject it. And also instead of wearing traditional ceremonial dress, they insisted on wearing new, Western-style clothing. All these sudden changes should be considered to be a great affront to our country and we are just being cautious about their weird behavior.

Hong Sunmok (洪淳穆, 判府事 chief minister-without-portfolio): Now we should establish friendly relations with neighboring countries and show our capacity for tolerance in dealing with other countries. And we should not be the first to cause an estrangement. Someone is saying that the *Sŏgye* is not acceptable because of some words in it, but an agreement has not yet been reached. (Hong seemed to agree with accepting the *Sŏgye*, though he gave no definite opinion about it.)

Kyusu: It is true that the deliberate changes in the new *Sŏgye* are really unappropriate. Nonetheless, it is difficult to accuse them of not keeping the comity of the *Kyorin* international society and to force them to address their king as a 'humble prince'. The Japanese have used the title 'Emperor' for several thousand years, when King P'yung (平) of the Chu (周) dynasty reigned in China. It is inevitable for the Japanese people to follow the old rules within their own country in order to show their respect for their King to the highest degree. It is not for us to criticize them for the way they handle their own affairs. All matters are up to you, Majesty, whether to accept it comprehensively or not. They are saying that they have finished carrying out their political reforms and now are making a bigger plan for rebuilding relations with their neighboring countries. Since their *Sŏgye* has been rejected for such a long time, I have a strong concern that they might develop increasing resentment, resulting in a bad impact for us .... Your Majesty could inquire from all ministers in this room what phrases or provisions in the *Sŏgye* are inappropriate.

Ch'oiŭng: We should not accept the *Sŏgye* because it came directly from the Japanese Ministry of Foreign Affairs without being passed through Tsushima. This was something that had never happened during the last 300 years. Also, they have altered the title of their king to a higher one, raising their own status in the process. Furthermore, they have altered the procedure of the banquet which was different from the previous time.

Pyŏngguk: It is proper to reject the *Sŏgye*, if one word of the contents were written against the protocol of the *Kyorin* order. Some phrases in the new *Sŏgye* cannot bear comparison with the previous one on numerous points. That is the very reason why we have persisted in refusing to accept it. Out of generosity for men coming from afar, a banquet was prepared for the Japanese envoys last time. But there arose a dispute, because they dressed in Western style costumes and insisted on entering through the main gate.[18] It is difficult to understand what their real intentions are. If we were to receive the new *Sŏgye* now, there would not be any estrangement between the two countries for the time being. But how can we be sure that they would not request something even more difficult for us to solve?

18) Under the established protocol, they should enter through the side gates.

Besides the dialogues above, SJWIL and ISN record the opinions of all the participants. Making a pretext of discretion, almost all of the ministers objected to the idea of receiving the *Sŏgye* and left King Kojong to decide by himself. At this meeting almost all of the ministers also avoided their responsibility by saying that they could not give any definite opinion.[19]

Finally, King Kojong ordered everyone to write down their own opinions, but the King's order was not executed because of the objection of Yi Yuwŏn and Kim Pyŏngguk.

At the end, the participants decided to have another meeting and to inform King Kojong of their decisions. They therefore presented a memorial to the Throne that Korea should not receive the *Sŏgye* for three reasons: first, the Japanese Ministry of Foreign Affairs directly delivered the *Sŏgye* without passing through Tsushima; second, that it was not written with modesty and politeness, according to the rules of the *Kyorin* order; and last, the procedure of the banquet was absolutely different from that used in the past.[20]

However, they decided to send a translator to negotiate with the Japanese counterpart. Kim Kyeun (金繼運) was selected as a special translator to negotiate with Moriyama.[21] But the acute problems between the two countries could not be solved by sending low-level officials such as translators. While one side

19) SJWIL, 5, pp. 245-246; ISN, 70, pp. 875-880; KJSL, 1, p. 498.
20) See the memorial of the Council of the State, ISN, 70, p. 883; KJSL, 1, p. 498.
21) KJSL, 1, p. 501, 503.

strongly upheld the *Kyorin* order, the other justified itself for seeking to destroy it. Thereby, the relationship between the two countries came to a deadlock.

After the royal meeting of June 13, 1875, Pak Kyusu sent a letter to the Taewŏngun, the leader of the conservatives. Pak wrote that all the people at the conference wanted to accept the *Sŏgye* in their mind, but they could not express their real intention for fear of personal troubles in the future. Pak also judged that Japan had already taken military action, for they had dispatched gunboats to the Korean shore under the pretext of escorting their envoys. He raised doubts about sending a translator to deliver a protest to the Japanese envoys and examine the words of the new *Sŏgye* in every detail. Lastly he warned that, after hearing the cannon fire, it was impossible to accept the *Sŏgye* and to restore good relations with Japan.[22]

In another letter to Yi Ch'oeŭng, the chief state councillor, Pak vented his pent-up feelings towards all the ministers and their poor spirited behavior at the conference:

> How imprudent it is, at the banquet held at the office of the Prefect of Tongrae, to find fault with the Japanese envoys because they were wearing Western dress instead of the traditional costumes of the past, and to create such useless disputes!
>
> Our court decided to send a translator. Then, where would he go? Should he go to Tsushima? Or to Tokyo? If he were in Tokyo, what

---

22) Pak's letter (1)-(c). Such political atmosphere is vividly depicted in the dialogue between O Kyŏngsŏk (吳慶錫) and Moriyama on February 13, 1876, which will be explained later.

would he discuss?

Should our translator ask for the restoration of our relationship with Tsushima? Furthermore, the Tongrae Prefect is only an official of a province and how could he dare answer whether the new *Sŏgye* should be accepted or not?[23]

Pak's judgement that Japan was going to take military action was correct. Japan recalled Moriyama and decided to turn to military measures. The so-called *Unyo* Incident (雲揚號) was shortly to break out.

---

23) Pak's letter (2)-(d).

3

Transformation of the *Kyorin* Order

__ Japanese Gunboat Diplomacy

__ Political Background of the Kanghwa Incident

__ Negotiation between Japan and China: The Suzerainty Problem

__ Negotiation of the Treaty of Amity and Commerce between Korea and
Japan

Signed in February 1876, the Kwanghwa Treaty between Korea and Japan led to the dissolution of the Kyorin order. In that sense, it marked a turning point in Far Eastern diplomatic history. Japan began to deeply infiltrate in Korean politics, whereas China continued to be eager to maintain her traditional position on the Korean peninsula. Finally, the Western powers decided to undertake a diplomatic démarche in order to conclude a treaty with Korea. It is therefore important to analyze the international perception of the Korean court during those turbulent years.

Japanese Gunboat Diplomacy

Moriyama Shigeru (森山茂) and Hirotsu Hironobu (廣津弘信) became indignant at Korea's policy. On April 23, 1875, Hirotsu submitted a report to the Japanese government titled 'A

Proposition for the Dispatch of Gunboats in Order to Promote Negotiations.' In that report, Hirotsu proposed that as the seclusionist forces of the Taewŏnkun and his entourage were weakening, it was the right time to carry out a swift military demonstration. He concluded that because of the political turmoil in the Korean court, a small scale military demonstration would have a great effect. This proposal highlights Japanese attitudes of that time and the salient parts are as follows:

> Now, this is the right moment for us to show our power. I am asking for the use of force, because it is sufficient to achieve our goal with the simple display of one or two military ships in Korean waters. My proposal aims at the prevention of the possibilities of great troubles in the future and not to intimidate the neighboring country with arms. I need your prompt decision.[1]

On September 3, since the negotiations continued to be deadlocked, the Japanese government decided to recall Moriyama. Hirotsu had already returned to Japan and the only thing left was the use of force.

Upon Moriyama's return to Japan, the Japanese government carried out its military plan, which is now called as the Kanghwa Incident (江華島 事件) or the *Unyo* Incident (雲揚號 事件). As to the unfolding of this incident, a great deal of research has been produced by Korean and Japanese academics.[2] Therefore, in this

---

1) NGB, 8, doc. no. 29, p. 72.
2) See the bibliography at Yongkoo Kim (1996), pp. 87-117.

book, only the important characteristics and aspects of the incident will be examined.

Before the outbreak of the *Unyo* Incident, the Japanese government decided, in accordance with Hirotsu's proposal, to send three gunboats to Pusan. Accordingly, the *Unyo* arrived in Pusan on May 25. When Hyŏn Sŏkun, the Korean language official, asked the reason of her coming, the *Unyo* crew gave the prepared answer that they came to protect their envoys and also to determine the reasons for the rejection of the Japanese *Sŏgye*. When Hyŏn's group climbed aboard the *Unyo*, she opened fire under the pretext of conducting a military exercise. Three gunboats including the *Unyo* then returned to Japan for a time.[3]

But the *Unyo* again appeared in Korean waters in September. She reached Kanghwa Island on September 19 under the pretext of heading to Newchang (牛莊). A group of crew members including the captain sailed in a boat up to the islands strait, which led to the Han River, as an excuse to find a supply of fresh water. It was, in fact, a deliberate act of provocation. The batteries of the Ch'oji fortress (草芝鎭) had no choice but to fire and the *Unyo* promptly returned fire.

After attacking Ch'oji Fortress, the *Unyo* went to Yŏngjong Island (永宗島), off Incheon, plundered it in retaliation, and killed thirty-five men. The Japanese forces captured 16 men, took 36 cannons and 130 guns as loot, and returned to Nagasaki on September 28. This incident is called the *Unyo* or the Kanghwa Incident.

---

3) NGB, 8, an addition of doc. no. 36, pp. 92-94.

But today nobody believes the reliability of Japanese sources, such as 『Jiyutoshi (自由黨史)』, which insists that the *Unyo*'s decision to call at Kanghwa Island was in order to get fresh water.[4] Nowadays, it is commonly accepted that the *Unyo* Incident was preplanned by the Japanese Navy, whose top members were from the Satsuma clan (薩摩藩).

First of all, let us examine the report of Lieutenant Commander Inoue Yoshika (井上良馨), the captain of the *Unyo*. Upon his return to Japan, he reported the incident on October 8 and the following is his outline of events:

> I was ordered to investigate the route from the southeastern sea of Korea to Newchang, China. When I arrived near Kanghwa Island, I predetermined that we were short of fresh water and we could not sail to Newchang. We anchored at Wŏlmi Island (月尾島) off Incheon on September 19. The next day, we set off to Kanghwa Island and anchored the boat pointing toward Ŭng Island (鷹島). From there, we transferred into a small boat and had sailed up the southern part of Kanghwa Island and arrived around the third battery. When we sailed up along the strait for a long time, we arrived at Ch'oji fortress and, there, we were attacked.[5]

In this report, there is something very unconvincing. Fresh water was the most important provision in sailing and it was unbelievable that one would 'predetermine' the amount of water.

---

4) Yamabe (1970, pp. 26-29) severely criticizes the records of 『Jiyutoshi』 and Tabohashi's interpretation relying upon such sources.
5) NGB, 8, enclosure 1 of doc. no. 57, pp. 686-687.

They could have gotten a supply of water at Tsushima or Pusan, and the itinerary from Nagasaki to Newchang was not a long journey and it was hard to believe that they were short of water when they came near Kanghwa Island.

Furthermore the *Unyo* had not been supplied with any fresh water from its departure from Kanghwa Island on September 20, till the 28th when they arrived at Nagasaki.[6]

In the biography of Yamagata Aritomo (山縣有朋), who was the founder of the modern Japanese army, the Kanghwa Incident was vividly described as a prearranged plan by the Satsuma (薩摩) clan in the Navy. Let us look at the paragraphs of Yamagata's diary connected with the Kanghwa Incident.

> The answer to the Korean question was interrupted because of the breakdown of the dispatch of envoys to Korea and the resignation of Saigo Takamori (西鄉隆盛), but in the Navy there were many Saigo followers who strongly stirred up 'arguments over whether to conquer Korea' in order to solve the problems between the two countries.
>
> The military demonstration of Captain Inoue of the *Unyo* on the Korean shore in 1875 was accomplished under a tacit agreement with Kawamura Smiyoshi (川村純義), the Vice-Minister of the Navy.
>
> In September 1875, Inoue was ordered on a secret mission to demonstrate military force to Korea, under the pretext of investigating a sea-route to Newchang in China. Accordingly, when the news of the incident was reported to the Japanese government, it was not a surprise for the Japanese Navy because the preplanned

---

6) Yamabe (1970), pp. 29-30.

adventure had been accomplished.[7]

Political Background of the Kanghwa Incident

This incident was a manifestation of the typical Japanese attitude towards Korea. The essence of the age-old Japanese policy was that if pourparler and mediation fail, one should immediately resort to force. Especially after the Meiji Reformation, the policy toward Korea was closely connected with Japan's own internal political situation. As far as Korean issues were concerned, they were, in a sense, treated as domestic matters.

Seikanron was nothing but a pretext for resolving internal discontents, as well as to unite national opinion by taking advantage of an external crisis. Such arguments over whether to conquer Korea had arisen before the *Sŏgye* question was on the agenda between Korea and Japan.

Nevertheless, the arguments came to the fore around 1873. Samurai groups lost their positions overnight when the government decreed the 'Imperial Rescript on the Abolition of the Clan' in 1871 and the 'Notification of Conscription Act' in 1872.

The number of such jobless Samurais reached 600,000 men, and how to deal with them was one of the difficulties faced by the Meiji government.[8] *Seikanron* was nothing but one remedy for this internal question.

---

7) Tokutomi (1933), vol. 2, ch. 11.
8) Yamabe (1970), p. 10.

Therefore, the faction opposed to *Seikanron* never denied the necessity of invading Korea, but quarrelled with the *Seikanron* faction over the timing of the proposed invasion. It should be remembered that the beginning of modern relations between Korea and Japan was closely connected to internal political maneuvers in Japan.

The Kanghwa Incident could not be abandoned as a simple Japanese military demonstration. The incident became a serious international problem, largely because Japan decided to solve the Korean question in one coup. As the latter problem was closely intermingled with the *Sadae* order, Japan had to negotiate with China.

Negotiation between Japan and China: The Suzerainty Problem

At first, Japan had to make contact with the Chinese government. Thus, on October 5, 1875, Kido Takayoshi (木戸孝允), the Cabinet Councilor (参議), submitted a proposal[9] to Sanjo Sanetomi, the Prime Minister (太政大臣), regarding the negotiations with China.

Kido's opinion was that Japan should press China, the suzerain power, to assume responsibility over the Korean matter. If China decided not to do so, Japan would then deal directly with Korea.

---

9) NGSS, 1, pp. 14-16.

Following Kido's advice, the Japanese government decided to set up a research committee on the Korean question, a committee composed of Ito Hirobumi (伊藤博文), Inoue Kowashi (井上毅), and G. E. Boissonade. This committee also concluded that envoys should be sent to Korea and to China in order to clearly determine the Chinese attitude towards Korea.[10]

The Meiji government finally decided to send Mori Arinori (森有禮) to China. On November 20, 1875, he received instructions from Terashima Munenori (寺島宗則), the Minister of Foreign Affairs, which ran as follows:

> It is uncertain that the Kanghwa Incident had occurred according to the plan of the Korean government, or if it was an arbitrary decision of its provincial officials. Therefore, Japan will dispatch an envoy to Korea in order to discuss compensation and to restore the old friendly relations with Korea. Japan will do her best in relations with China.[11]

The Chinese government had already learnt the outline of the incident through Tei Einei (鄭永寧), the acting Japanese Minister to China, on October 13, and saw the possible causes of the incident as follows:

(1) Did Japan despise Koreans? Did the premeditated design of the Japanese make Koreans enraged?
(2) Did the Western powers, which had failed in their negotiations

---

10) NGSS, 1, doc. no. 3, pp. 4-8.
11) NGB, 8, doc. no. 61, pp. 139-140.

with Korea, instigate the Japanese to make the incident?

(3) Was the Japanese government led by people who advocated the invasion of Korea?[12]

The Zongli Yamen (總理衙門) correctly foresaw the most significant aspects of the Kanghwa Incident.

Mori arrived in Peking on January 5, 1876 and he had his first meeting with Chinese officials on January 10, at around 2 p.m. The Chinese representatives, Shen Guifen (沈桂芬), Dong Xun (董恂), Chong Hou (崇厚) and Guo Songtao (郭嵩燾), explained the tributary system in detail and said that even though Korea was a vassal, she was autonomous in government exhortations and restrictions (政教禁令). Mori asked whether 'government exhortations and restrictions' included foreign relations. Shen Guifen answered in the affirmative.

From this time on, Japan began to claim that Korea was an independent state, being autonomous in domestic and external affairs, and that the Chinese assertion of suzerainty was a non-issue.[13]

Mori also requested a Chinese explanation concerning the Korean question in written form. In response, on January 14, Prince Kung (恭親王) sent Mori a dispatch explaining that Korea, being a Chinese territory, came under Article 1 of the Treaty of

---

12) ZRJS, 1, p. 1, enclosure 1 of doc. no. 1. The Zongli Yamen's Memorial dated Jan. 17, 1876 (Lunar Dec. 21, 1875).

13) ZRJS, 1, enclosures 1-7 of doc. no. 2, pp. 2-4; NGB, 9, doc. no. 39, pp. 142-162, doc. no. 41, 42, pp. 153-167.

Peace, Commerce and Navigation concluded between China and Japan in 1871. That article stipulated that "in all that regards the territorial possessions of either country the two governments shall treat each other with proper courtesy." Hence, the two sides exchanged communications refuting each other's viewpoints.

The Korean question could not be resolved with a mere oral discussion. China insisted on maintaining the *Sadae* order of the Confucian world, while Japan, on the other hand, heralded the order of Western international law.

Mori prided himself as a specialist in international law, but Dong Xun and Guo Songtao had also reached the highest standards in the field of Western international law. Mori also understood the *Sadae* order well, but he was only searching for justification for conducting direct negotiations with Korea and to avoid the interference of China. This was therefore a typical example of the clash of the *Sadae* and the order of Western international law.

Although Mori participated in extensive discussions concerning the Korean matter with the Zongli Yamen's officials, he contrived to meet the most influential person in China, Li Hungchang (李鴻章), and to press for an appropriate answer for Japan.

The Zongli Yamen advised Li not to meet Mori, but Li himself volunteered to meet him.[14] Li, a 53 year-old veteran politician, wanted to persuade Mori, a 30 year-old young diplomat. On January 24 and 25, 1876, Li met Mori at Tientsin and Baodingpu.[15]

---

14) LGCC, 5, p. 104.

15) Li held dual positions. His office of Superintendent for the Northern Ports (北洋大臣) was located at Tientsin and his another office of Governor of

Li asked the reason why the Japanese ship had penetrated deep into the shore of Kanghwa Island, since it was forbidden to enter within 10 *li* (里) of the other nation's shores according to Mankuokongfa (萬國公法, Public Law of All Nations). Mori answered that the ship only wanted fresh drinking water, but the Korean Army, despite recognizing the Japanese flag on the ship, had fired at it.

Mori also insisted that China and Japan could invoke Mankuokongfa, but Korea could not do so, because Korea did not conclude treaties with foreign states. Mori emphasized that Japan wanted only two things: (1) Korea should show the appropriate courtesy to Japan, and (2) Japanese ships should be protected in Korean waters.

The discussions between Li and Mori ran in a parallel line, because Li repeatedly emphasized that he followed the Zongli Yamen's stance regarding Korea's vassalage.[16] Mori finally came to know straight from Li's own mouth about the firm Chinese posture. China, as a suzerain power, felt a strong moral responsibility towards Korea, even though Korea exercised full autonomy in internal and external affairs. Mori decided that it was wise to close negotiations with China in due course.

Li Hungchang was in the difficult position at that time. China was embroiled in serious conflicts with England arising from the Margary Incident, and at the same time with France regarding the

---

Chili Province (直隸總督) at Baodingpu (保定府).

16) ZRJS, 1, enclosure 8 of doc. no. 2, pp. 4-5; NGB, 9, doc. no. 45 pp. 169-180.

Vietnamese question. She could not deal with a new conflict with Japan. In these circumstances, Li thought that if Korea concluded a treaty with Japan, a military confrontation between Korea and Japan could be avoided.

Li therefore came to the conclusion that Korea should accept the Japanese demands. On January 19, 1876, before he met Mori, Li had already communicated such a conclusion to the Zongli Yamen.[17]

While Li and Mori were having a heated theoretical discussion concerning the Korean matter, life-and-death negotiations were underway on Kanghwa Island.

Negotiation of the Treaty of Amity and Commerce between Korea and Japan

After the Kanghwa Incident, Japan was temporarily unable to take any definite actions towards Korea due to its own internal political crisis. Moriyama, in Korea during the Kanghwa Incident, returned to Japan on November 3, 1875, and the next day he submitted a report to the Minister of Foreign Affairs. In this report, Moriyama presented extensive details about internal affairs in Korea and strongly recommended that envoys be sent to Korea to demand responsibility for the Kanghwa Incident.[18] In response, the Japanese government finally decided to take action towards

---

17) LGCC, 5, p. 104.
18) NGB, 8, doc. no. 58, pp. 133-137.

Korea.

On December 9, the government appointed Kuroda Kiyotaka (黑田淸隆), the Exploration Commissioner (開拓長官) and Cabinet Councilor, as an envoy extraordinary and minister plenipotentiary, and Inoue Kaoru (井上馨), Senate Councilor (元老院 議官), as an associate envoy. They were thus sent to Kanghwa Island with six ships and three hundred soldiers. Hirotsu had already informed the Korean government of the dispatch of the envoys to Kanghwa Island.

As soon as Kuroda's party arrived at Pusan on January 15, 1876, Yamanojo Skenaga (山之城祐長), the Acting Chief of the Japan House announced Kuroda's arrival to Yi Chunsu (李濬秀), the assistant language officer, and began to threaten him.

> The Japanese minister is going to Kanghwa Island to negotiate with Korea. If the Korean high officials do not appear at the meeting, our officials will go directly to Seoul. They will arrive on Kanghwa Island in seven or eight days.[19]

In fact, Japan began by demonstrating its military force. On January 17, 1876, Kuroda wrote in his diary as follows:

> Around noon, before going to Kanghwa Island, four ships, the *Nitsin* (日進), the *Mosung* (孟春), the *Hakodate* (函館) and the *Kyoru* (矯龍), fired ten cannons and conducted naval exercises. I saw many Koreans gathered on the banks in order to see our demonstration.[20]

---

19) KJSL, 1, p. 513.
20) NGB, 9, addition 1 of doc. no. 3, p. 9.

After the military drill, they left Pusan for Kanghwa Island, on January 23. When the *Nitsin* was anchored at Taepu Island (大阜島), off Incheon, on January 30, O Kyŏngsŏk (吳慶錫), an official with the rank above upper-senior third grade at the Office of Interpreters (司譯院), and Hyŏn Sŏkun (玄昔運), the language officer, appeared at 9:30 a.m.

The dialogue among O, Hyŏn, Miyamoto, and Moriyama was so important that we will examine it later. After receiving the report from O, the Korean government appointed Sin Hŏn (申櫶), Commanding General of Ŏyŏng Regiment (御營大將),[21] as Minister of Reception (接見大臣) and Yun Chasŭng (尹滋丞), Deputy Commander of Military Headquarters (都總府 副摠管), as Vice Minister.

On February 5 and 6, preliminary negotiations were held between Yun and Moriyama at the office of the Kanghwa magistrate. From the beginning of these preliminary meetings, Japan began to make threats. Let us look at the scene of the meeting on the 5th:

> Moriyama: 4000 Japanese soldiers were going to come, but I brought only 400 soldiers because your country would not provide places for them to stay.
>
> Yun: Four hundred soldiers are far too many, because we don't have any sufficiently large quarters in which the soldiers could stay. I advise you to reduce the numbers.
>
> Moriyama: There is a protocol for the envoys about how many

---

21) One of the Five Military Commands (五衛).

soldiers can be brought with them. Therefore, I cannot reduce the number of soldiers. Soon, two thousand soldiers will follow and you would be well advised to provide places for them to camp at Incheon and Pup'yŏng (富平).

Yun: This meeting of the delegates is going to reestablish our old amiable relationship. Why do you need so many soldiers? .... I cannot understand the reason why your soldiers are going to land in Incheon and at Pup'yŏng.[22]

Sin Hŏn and Kuroda met for the first time on February 10, 1876. On that day, Kuroda called on Sin Hŏn at 3:40 p.m. only to pay his respects.

The next day the meeting started in earnest. At the Military Training Camp (練武臺) in the Kanghwa magistracy, the meeting continued from 1:00 to 5:00 p.m. regarding the Kanghwa Incident, full powers, and the *Sŏgye* problems. Let us examine part of the dialogue between Sin and Kuroda:

Sin: It is a grand event to promote our three-hundred-year-old friendship today.

Kuroda: The purpose of our visit was already cited in general in Hirotsu's letter. Last year, our ship, the *Unyo*, was fired on by your border soldiers and how could you mention our old courtesy of the *Kyorin* that we shared for such a long time?

Sin: It's clarified in the Liching (禮經) that to enter the boundaries of any country is strictly forbidden. Our soldiers could not recognize why the foreign ship was crossing over the boundary line and also did not know the nationality of the ship.

---

22) YHHN, 4, pp. 336-338, 340-341; NGB, 9, doc. no. 13, pp. 58-65.

Furthermore, as the ship intruded deep into the defending forts, our guards had to fire.

Kuroda: How could it be possible for your soldiers not to know the nationality of the *Unyo*? There were three masts with our flags on them.

Sin: You had yellow flags on at that time and the soldiers thought that they were not Japanese flags.

Kuroda: We have already let you know about our flags, so why did you not notify all districts about them?

Sin: Last time, your soldiers anchored at Yŏng Chong Island off Incheon and plundered the place. That was against the *Kyorin* order. Historically, we have been kind to wrecked ships. So, why would we fire only upon your ship?

Kuroda: In our negotiations, could you decide with full discretion?

Sin: Your officials have full power to negotiate, but ours do not. I have to report every question to our court before reaching a decision.

After such dialogue, Japanese envoys began to condemn Korea for the rejection of the new *Sŏgye*. Sin Hŏn answered that it was because of Hachinohe's (八戶順叔) article, published in a Chinese newspaper in the fourth year of the reign of King Kojong, in 1867, that criticized the Korean court.[23]

As a matter of fact, that article had created quite a stir in Korea. The Korean court knew of its existence when the Chinese Ministry of Rites secretly reported foreign information, including that article, to the Korean Board of Rites, on March 20, 1867. The information, consisting of five points, is as follows:

23) KJSL, 1, p. 515; YHHN, 4, pp. 343-348; NGB, 9, doc. no. 16, pp. 80-87.

(1) The gist of Hachinohe's article: Nowadays, Japan is in the midst of military preparations and possesses eighty military ships. She is intent on conquering Korea. Korea was a tributary country of Japan in the past, but Korea has abolished the tributary system. Therefore, Japan is going to punish her.

(2) Previously France withdrew its army from Korea as the winter season came. But she is going to invade Korea again in the spring. So will Japan.

(3) Recently, 260 feudal lords held a political meeting in Tokyo and opinions were expressed about conquering Korea.

(4) A report from Chefoo: An American ship will sail to Korea in order to investigate the shipwreck which occurred previously. England, the U.S., and France are willing to go to Korea in the spring and they demand the establishment of commercial relations.

(5) In contrast to France, England is not going to attack Korea. The French government is not satisfied with the last Korean invasion.[24]

Nevertheless, the first meeting between Korea and Japan was a sort of a mild discussion and it finished without a big confrontation. But the second meeting, held on February 12, from 2:00 to 5:45 p.m., was of a very different character. At the beginning of the meeting, Kuroda mentioned, quoting the *Sŏgye* problems, that because of the refusal to receive the Japanese envoys, nationwide opinion was in favor of punishing Korea, but the Japanese government had appeased the public's wrath. Such an utterance was an obvious threat to Korea. Kuroda added that

---

24) TMHG, 3, pp. 2479-2481.

he had to report to his government when he returned home.

When Sin Hŏn asked what Kuroda was going to report to the Japanese government, Kuroda finally revealed the core of the problem.[25] Kuroda presented the draft articles of a treaty with Korea and Sin Hŏn retorted as follows:

> Korea is situated at the extremes of the seas and is only defending herself. She is ignorant about recent international affairs. Our land is bewildered [and is not rich enough to produce any products]. Therefore, we never accumulate enough products for trade. We only produce grain and cotton, which cannot be the means of trading with foreign countries. Rather it will bring dissatisfaction to both countries.[26]

Nevertheless, Kuroda rejected Sin Hŏn's opinion and insisted that to conclude a treaty was a principle of the 'Public Law of All Nations (萬國公法).' Sin Hŏn finished the meeting by saying that he would report the matter to the Korean court.

The third and the last meeting was held on February 13, from 1:00 to 3:00 p.m. Kuroda and his party demanded an answer within ten days, otherwise Japan would be obliged to resort to military measures. We are going to look at the threatening scene of that particular day:

> Kuroda: It is unnecessary to continue the meeting any longer [if Korea does not accept the treaty] ... If the treaty were not

---

25) NGB, 9, doc. no. 17, pp. 87-92.
26) KJSL, 1, p. 516.

accomplished this time, this would be a tragedy for both countries and an unexpected incident would arise in the future .... Probably, our army would land in your country .... Only if your court decided to apologize and to repent, we could report the fact to our government.

Sin Hŏn: We have met here in order to restore the old friendship between the two countries and you are threatening me every minute with the use of military force. This is against the courtesy of *li* (禮) .... And how could you dare make your soldiers land in a foreign country without our permission?[27]

After the meeting, Sin Hŏn reported to the court that Korea should be more cautious towards Japan than before. He added that the Japanese were changing their attitude frivolously and threatening us all the time. On the other hand, the Korean court informed Sin Hŏn, on February 18, that it was necessary to continue discussing a treaty with Japan. The following day, the Korean court gave Sin Hŏn full powers, that is, 'the discretionary power to decide', and notified him of the Korean counter-proposal. Thus, the meeting was underway rapidly, but unexpectedly came to a deadlock because of the ratification problem.

On February 20, the Japanese requested King Kojong's signature for ratification and insisted that such a signature was required according to the Common Law of All Nations (萬國普通之法). Sin Hŏn and Yun Chasŭng replied that it was impossible to ask for the royal signature for ratification and only the royal signature of one

---

27) KJSL, 1, p. 517.

word 'YUN (允)' [meaning Royal permission] was sufficient. At this point, Kuroda made a threatening gesture and left Kanghwa Island for the time being, leaving everything to Inoue. Henceforth, Sin Hŏn negotiated with Inoue and Miyamoto several times and they finally agreed that Korea would mint a new seal inscribed as the 'Seal of the Korean King' and use it instead of the royal signature. The ratification would be exchanged at the same time as the conclusion of the treaty. Thereby, on February 27, 1876, the historic treaty between Korea and Japan was signed at the Military Training Camp on Kanghwa Island.

4

Contents of the Treaty between Korea and Japan

This treaty was the first international agreement Korea ever concluded under the legal formalities of Western international law. But Korea and Japan interpreted its contents quite differently for a considerable length of time. In addition, this treaty was not sufficient in its contents to solve the acute issues arising from the clash between the Kyorin *order and Western international law. Nevertheless, as a result of this treaty the* Kyorin *order, one of the two pillars of Korean international relations, had begun to collapse.*

The contents of the treaty will be explained along with the 13 articles proposed by the Japanese on February 12 and the Korean counter-proposal issued on February 19.[1]

---

1) For the contents of the Korean counter-proposal, see WSIG, Jan. 25 (lunar), 1876; ISMJ, Jan. 25, 26 (lunar), 1876; NGB, 9, doc. no. 20, pp. 97-99, Tabohashi (1940), 1, pp. 472-477.

The purpose of the treaty was briefly stated in the Preamble as follows:

> Amity has existed since ancient times between Great Korea and Great Japan. But their relations never having been clearly defined, it has been thought desirable to base them upon more solid foundations, so that they may stand forever.

The first Japanese draft used the terms 'His Excellency the Korean King,' and 'His Excellency the Emperor of Great Japan.' The word 'Great' was used only for the Japanese part. Consequently, Korean envoys raised an objection against the unilateral use of the word 'great.' They also insisted on using the nations' names instead of the sovereign's titles. The Koreans quoted as an example the treaty between China and England. Finally, the Korean objections were accepted by the Japanese.

In Article I, Korea was designated as an autonomous state (自主之邦). This article provoked serious problems between the two countries in subsequent times and it clearly shows the extreme differences between the two countries' worldviews. The gist of the article reads as follows:

> Chosŏn, being an autonomous state, enjoys equal rights with Japan .... All old rules and precedents which have in the past been found vexatious to the opposite party shall be and are hereby abrogated ....

Many scholars have claimed that with this article Korea and

Japan agreed upon the dissolution of the *Sadae-Kyorin* order. But such an interpretation should be guarded against. First of all, it should be remembered that this article never used terms like 'sovereignty', or 'sovereign', and only defined Korea as an autonomous state. 'Autonomy' was a concept accepted under the *Sadae* order and 'sovereignty' was a political word used in Western international law order.

Under the *Sadae* order, *waifan* (外藩) has complete 'autonomy' over internal affairs, even though *waifan*'s matters, in principle, fall under the jurisdiction of the Chinese Board of Rites. But from the middle of 1870s, Chinese authorities began to concede that *waifan* also had 'autonomy' over external matters. One can easily surmise that 'autonomy' is a quite different concept from 'independence', which means 'sovereignty' in Western international law order.

The Japanese equated 'autonomy' with 'independence', and Korea therefore became a 'sovereign state' in terms of Western international law; the *Sadae* order thereby dissolved automatically. The Koreans, by contrast, interpreted 'autonomy' in the first article as a continuing concept under the *Sadae* order. Such a clash also existed in the conflict between the orders of the Middle Ages and of modern times in Western diplomatic history. During the Vienna Conference in 1814~15, the discussion between 'Sovereignty' and 'Landeshoheit' is a good example.[2]

This clash surrounding the first article continued for some time

---

2) Yongkoo Kim (1997, a), p. 35, 104.

and it created a conflict between the two countries, a rift which will be discussed in the next chapter. In addition, the two countries also differed in the interpretation of the latter part of the article, which regulated abrogation of the rules detrimental to their relations. Korea interpreted this to mean abrogation of the rules that were harmful to the continuation of the *Kyorin* order, whereas Japan understood that this order was no longer operational from that time on.

A reciprocal dispatch of envoys was stipulated in Article II as follows:

> Within fifteen months of the date of this treaty the Japanese will send a representative to the capital of Korea, where he shall be permitted to communicate freely with the Minister of the Board of Rites in order to arrange all the details of mutual friendly intercourse between the two countries. The Japanese representative shall be free at all times to remain in Korea or return to Japan at will. The government of Korea may also at any future time send its representative to Tokyo, the capital of Japan, and there he may communicate freely with the Minister of the Foreign Office in order to arrange all affairs of mutual concern between the two countries. The representative of Korea shall also be free to remain in Japan or to return at his pleasure.

This article clearly reflects the clash between the *Koryin* order and the order of Western international law. Japan considered that by this stipulation the system of permanent envoys was established. On the other hand, Korea regarded this article as a continuation of the traditional envoy system (Tongsinsa, 通信使) under the *Koryin* order system.

The present system of permanent ambassadors is the core of the modern international law system, whereas, under the *Kyorin* system a Tongsinsa was dispatched only on specific occasions to Edo (Tokyo), where they stayed in general for fifteen days. The tension between the two countries arising from their conflicting interpretation of the second article continued until 1880.

The instruction Kuroda received stated as follows:

> In order to enhance reciprocal friendship, envoys shall be stationed in the capitals of either country. This envoy shall enjoy the same status as the Minister of the Board of Rites.[3]

Kuroda was obviously ordered by the Japanese government to establish a system of permanent envoys. But he failed to fully carry out these instructions. Kuroda's first proposal was of unequal import and ambiguous in its regulation. He proposed that within fifteen months of the conclusion of the treaty, a Japanese envoy should be dispatched to Seoul where he would meet a minister, while a Korean envoy in Tokyo would meet a high official in the Ministry of Foreign Affairs. He further proposed that such envoys would be allowed to stay in the capitals of either country or to return home after negotiations.

Korea strongly opposed Kuroda's proposal. The gist of the Korean counter-proposal was that if a Korean envoy in Tokyo met only a high official, while a Japanese envoy in Seoul met a minister, it would be against international equity. Such Korean

---

3) NGB, 8, doc. no. 61, p. 116.

opposition was readily accepted by Japan.

Korean protests continued. Once the ports were selected for opening and trade was ongoing between the two countries, the rest of the matters would be discussed between the provincial officials of the two countries. Therefore, diplomatic envoys did not need to stay in the capitals. The sea route being rough which made frequent visits unprofitable for either country, it was convenient to exchange envoys once every ten or fifteen years.

Finally Sin Hŏn and Miyamoto reached an agreement as it stood in Article II. But from Japan's point of view, the system of permanent envoys was not properly achieved because of the mistakes of Miyamoto. The stipulations in Article II contained many ambiguous points and would later create serious difficulties.

Article III was approved without any objections, as it stipulated technical contents. It reads as follows:

> In all written communications between the two countries, the Japanese government will write in its native language, giving therewith a translation into Chinese during the forthcoming ten years, and the Korean government shall write in Chinese.

Article IV which regulated trade, passage, and building houses in the treaty ports was agreed upon in the Japanese draft as follows:

> Trade having long been carried on between the Japanese and Koreans at the official residence of Japan at Ch'oryanghang (草梁項), in the harbor of Pusan, all the old rules and customs of that trade

shall be abolished and the new trade regulations in accordance with the articles and the stipulations of this treaty shall be provided. Subject to Article V below, Korea shall open two ports upon its coast which the Japanese may freely visit for purposes of trade, and where they may acquire land and build houses and stores, or rent houses from the Koreans.

But it was not an easy task to solve the concrete problems arising from this article. First of all, to set boundaries for how far the Japanese in the treaty ports could travel was an issue of the utmost difficulty. The Korean court was well aware that China permitted giving passports to foreigners, who went freely inland for trade, a fact which facilitated the infiltration of Western capitalism into Chinese society.

Therefore, Korea firmly insisted on a boundary limit not to exceed 10 *li* (里) according to the Korean calculation. This Korean position was clearly reflected in the Additional Articles (附錄) appended to this treaty which was signed on August 24, 1876.

The selection of the treaty ports was another difficult problem which made negotiations difficult. Furthermore, the stipulation of Article V was very ambiguous:

> Two harbors most suitable for trade shall be sought out on the coast of the five provinces, i.e., Kyŏnggi (京畿), Ch'ungchŏng (忠清) Chŏnra (全羅), Kyŏngnam (慶南) and Hamgyŏng (咸慶). After examination of these coasts the location shall be settled upon by mutual agreement. The opening of these ports to trade shall occur within twenty months from the second month of Byŏncha (丙子) according to the Korean calendar and the second month of the ninth

year of Meiji (明治) according to the Japanese calendar.

Kuroda was instructed to open two ports, that is, Pusan and Kanghwa or another place near Seoul.[4] But he was given wide discretionary powers to select treaty ports after his actual investigation in Korea. He finally selected Yŏnghŭng (永興) in Hamkyŏng Province.

In the Japanese draft, Yŏnghŭng was to be opened within fifteen months and one of the ports of Kyŏnggi, Ch'ungch'ŏng, Chŏnra or Kyŏngsang Provinces within twenty months. However, Korea strongly opposed opening Yŏnghŭng because the founding father of the Chosŏn dynasty was buried nearby. Korea also opposed opening a port in Kyŏnggi, Ch'ungchŏng or Chŏnra Provinces and they only proposed opening one of the appropriate ports in Kyŏngsang Province.

Thus the selection of the treaty ports became one of the acute problems between the two countries. Finally Wŏnsan (元山) port was opened in August 1879, and Incheon (仁川) in September 1883.

Article VI which regulated shipwrecks, by contrast, was agreed upon without any serious arguments. It runs as follows:

> Hereafter, when any Japanese vessel shall be in distress on the Korean coast, whether through bad weather or in want of fuel or food, and such ship shall be unable to reach either one of the open ports, it shall be permitted to enter any harbor or bay which may be

---

4) NGB, 8, doc. no. 64, p. 148.

at hand to seek shelter from the winds and waves, and buy whatever the crew may require, to repair any damage, or to buy fuel as may be required.

Article VII permitted Japan to survey the Korean coast, thereby infringing on Korean sovereignty over its territorial waters. This stipulation reads as follows:

> As there are on the coast of Korea many unknown rocks and reefs both above and under the water, Japanese ships shall therefore be permitted to survey all these coasts and make charts, so as to assure the ships of both nations safe navigation of the Korean waters by mariners of either nation.

From the turn of the nineteenth century, foreign ships frequently appeared on Korean waters, causing Korean officials to worry about the repercussions. Under such circumstances, it is very strange that Korea accepted such a poisonous article on February 1876 without any objection. The instruction of the Japanese Government was that "Any Japanese warships or trade ships may navigate and survey any place on Korean waters." But for fear of possible Korean objections, Kuroda was to decide the timing of navigation and surveying.[5]

The dispatch of Japanese consuls was agreed upon in Article VIII:

---

5) NGB, 8, doc. no. 64, p. 146, 148.

Hereafter, Japanese consuls shall be sent to the ports to be opened in Korea, to govern the people who shall go from Japan to trade or reside there. If at any time any trouble should arise between the people of the two nations, the Japanese consul shall consult with local Korean authorities and so settle all disputes by mutual agreement.

This article was concluded without any objection. Korea might have thought of this article as the continuation of the system of Japanese envoys in Pusan under the *Kyorin* order. Furthermore, this article stipulated the dispatch of Japanese consuls to Korea and did not mention anything about Korean consuls in Japan.

Complete free trade between the two countries was provided in Article IX:

Peace and amity having now been settled between the two countries, the people of either country may freely resort to the other country for purposes of trade and commerce, and officials of either country shall in no way interfere with, or obstruct, the trade of the one people with the other.

If the merchants of either country shall defraud those of the opposite country or neglect to pay their just dues, the officers of the delinquent nation shall examine and rectify the wrong, always providing that the government of either side is not responsible for the debts of its subjects.

The latter part of this article was inserted on the request of the Korean side. This article, together with a note exchanged between Cho Inhŭi (趙寅熙) and Miyamoto Koichi (宮本小一), made Korea an economically dependent state, as we shall see in the next chapter.

Consular jurisdiction, one of the main legal apparatuses of the Western expansion toward the non-Western world, was provided in Article X:

> If any Japanese subject living in an open port in Korea commits any crime against any Korean subject, he shall be judged by his own government. If any Korean subject commits any crime against any Japanese subject, he shall be judged by his own government. On either side, impartial judgment shall be given, according to the laws of the respective countries.

Kuroda, who did not receive any instruction about consular jurisdiction, inserted this clause on his own initiative.

China and Japan had to accept unilateral consular jurisdiction in their treaties with Western powers. Japan initiated a movement for the treaty revision and, in 1871, Japan finally succeeded in achieving bilateral consular jurisdiction. But when Japan concluded a treaty with China that same year, Japan tried to insert a clause by which only China would accept consular jurisdiction. Of course, Japan failed to accomplish this in the face of strong Chinese opposition.

Under such circumstances, Japan forced Korea to accept unilateral consular jurisdiction. Nonetheless, the Korean court perceived the unequal nature of the Japanese proposal. She counter-proposed to solve criminal problems between the subjects of the two countries through on-the-spot consultation of the officials of the two countries. Nevertheless, the Korean counter-proposal was not accepted.

Additional articles and commercial regulations were to be concluded. Article XI stipulated as follows:

> Peace being now established between the two countries, commercial regulations must be enacted for the convenience of merchants of either country, and what has been provided for in general in these articles must be considered in detail, for which purpose officials of both countries being duly appointed by their respective governments shall within six months from this date meet at the capital of Korea or at the city of Kanghwa to consult upon and settle all the necessary rules and regulations.

Korea opposed holding further meetings, since the details were agreed upon, but the Japanese continued to insist on inserting this clause. Accordingly, Additional Articles (附錄) and Trade Regulations (通商章程) were agreed upon and signed in August, as will be explained later.

Article XII was a provision of *bona fide* fulfillment of the treaty and was agreed upon without any obstacles. In the original Japanese draft, Article XII was a most-favored-nation clause. But Korea strongly opposed inserting such a clause, since, she claimed, Korea was not planning to negotiate any treaties with other powers in the future and that if Korea were to conclude a treaty with other foreign countries, it could not be done without Japanese mediation.[6] On this point, tellingly enough, Japan was persuaded by Korea's tactful logic.

---

6) NGB, 9, doc. no. 20, p. 99.

5

Korea and the Dissolution of the *Kyorin* Order

__ Meeting between O Kyŏngsŏk and Myamoto

__ Conference in the Korean Court — February 14, 1876

__ The Anti-Treaty Movement in Korea

__ Dispatch of a Korean Envoy to Japan

__ The Emergence of Russian Question in the Far East

__ Permanent Residence of Japanese Envoy in Seoul

__ Tariff-Free Trade

It was a tremendously difficult task for the contemporary Chosŏn court to separate itself from the Kyorin *order and to accept the system of Western international law. Considering the conservative political atmosphere of the Korean court in the mid 1870s, the turmoil in the court can be easily understood. The people who belonged to the enlightened party insisted on concluding a new treaty with Japan, and King Kojong aligned himself with them. Despite the difficult political situation, their efforts to normalize diplomatic relations with Japan should be highly evaluated.*

After the conclusion of the Kanghwa Treaty, the Chosŏn government was not fully successful in the process of sending its first envoy to Japan. This problem is connected with the evaluation of Kim Kisu. Nevertheless, this period clearly shows the differences between Korean and Japanese worldviews.

Meeting between O Kyŏngsŏk and Myamoto

On January 30, 1876, O Kyŏngsŏk (吳慶錫), Miyamoto and Moriyama had a long conversation relating to the establishment of a new treaty. O expressed his candid opinions about treaty matters and the contemporary political atmosphere of the Korean court. Since O's views are only recorded in Japanese sources, there is no way to check their full reliability.

According to the Japanese documents, O was said to have spoken his inner mind as follows: since he had been in charge of diplomatic relations with China and Japan for such a long time, he advised the Korean court on many occasions to open diplomatic relations with foreign countries. Otherwise, Korea would be isolated from the world. Moreover, he greatly deplored the rejection of the Japanese envoys and Hyŏn Sŏkun (玄昔運), the language officer, also repeatedly advised the court to receive Japanese envoys, but the Korean court was ignorant about the importance of the matter. The previous year the Korean court would have accepted the Japanese *Sŏgye* and if there had been any problems in the *Sŏgye*, the matters would have been rearranged. Even though the Taewŏngun had resigned, almost all the Korean ministers asked secretly for his opinion on the affairs of state.

Asking for secrecy, O Kyŏngsŏk even revealed that when an American ship previously came to Korean shores, he had counseled King Kojong to open diplomatic relations with America, but his proposal had not been accepted because the American ship had left so soon.

He said that he was called as 'a promoter of the opening of ports (開港家),' and his opinions were not accepted. Concerning the relationship with Japan, people thought that Korea could repulse the Japanese, as we had done with the Americans. Since the Japanese envoys could not negotiate with the provincial officials on Kanghwa Island, O asked for the date of their arrival because the court would deal with the matter.

O said that he knew the meaning of 'full powers' and added his opinion that in the near future the Western powers would come to Korea for trade and in that case Japanese good offices should be sought. He finally remarked that he was very pleased to share enlightened talks with an enlightened man.[1]

It is evident, based on this conversation, that people who advocated the normalization of diplomatic relations with Japan occupied a very isolated position in Korea.

Conference in the Korean Court — February 14, 1876

It was in such an atmosphere that the Korean court received the Japanese proposal of the Thirteen Articles on February 13. In order to discuss this matter, an important court meeting was held at the Hall of Political Affairs (修政殿) and not only former and present

---

1) NGB, 9, doc. no. 6, pp. 27-39; NGSS, 1, pp. 102-119.

state councilors, but also all the officials with the rank above upper-senior third grade (堂上官), were asked to attend the meeting.

This court meeting was held on King Kojong's command that the government should reach a final decision on treaty matters.

Yi Yuwŏn (李裕元), Former Chief State Councilor, said that government officials had, indeed, discussed the matter for a long time, but they considered that the Japanese attitudes and intentions were unreasonable and unacceptable. As usual, Yi maintained a prudent approach concerning the policy on Japan.

Next, Kim Byŏnghak (金炳學), Chief Minister of the Office of Royal Relatives (領敦寧府事), expressed his opinion against the concluding of a treaty with Japan; he argued that while the Japanese spoke of reestablishing the old friendly terms with Korea, their real aim was to cause estrangement.

Kim Byŏngguk (金炳國), the Third State Councilor (右議政), argued that the real intentions of the Japanese were unclear and proposed an opinion that the court should decide what to do after receiving sufficient reports from Pusan.

Yi Ch'oiŭng (李最應), the Chief State Councilor (領議政), proposed a dilatory policy as the Japanese real intention had not yet been revealed and that afterwards the government should decide upon adequate measures against Japan.

It was only Pak Kyusu (朴珪壽), Chief Minister of the Office of Senior Officials without Portfolio (判中樞府事), who insisted on the inevitable conclusion of the treaty. He also said that since the Japanese delegates announced themselves as envoys of friendship we could not attack them first.[2]

Concerning such an important court meeting, documents retained in SJWIG, ISN, and KJSL were incredibly short and inadequate. After this court meeting, the Korean government rapidly changed its policy on Japan and opted to conclude the treaty.

The so-called 'Enlightenment Party' whose core members were Pak Kyusu, O Kyŏngsŏk, Hyŏn Sŏkun, Sin Hŏn (申櫶) and Kang Wi (姜瑋), pressed the government to adopt a new policy.

Kang Wi, who participated in the meeting on Kanghwa Island as a guard (伴倘) of Sin Hŏn, sent Pak Kyusu a letter, which stated the following: what Japan wants is to trade and if their demands are not accepted, they will use force. We should not attack them first, or make any sort of fault on our part, because if they were to land in Incheon or Pup'yŏng, they could easily enter Seoul and it would be very difficult to defend our capital in that case. Kang Wi added that, as a military man, he could state with certainty that the Korean army was too weak to stand up against Japanese military forces.[3]

On February 18, the Korean court finally ordered Sin Hŏn to conclude the treaty with Japan and the following day Sin Hŏn was given 'discretion to decide according to circumstances (隨事裁斷)', that is, 'full powers (全權)'.

On the 20th, Sin Hŏn was handed the Korean counter-proposal,

---

2) SJWIG, 5, pp. 500-501; ISN, 71, p. 201; KJSL, 1, p. 517.
3) KWCJ, pp. 519-523. For the Kang's activities, see Yi Kwangrin (1979), pp. 2-44.

which was already explained in Chapter 3. Along with this counter-proposal, the Korean court notified Sin Hŏn of the 'Six Principles' of negotiations, the contents of which were as follows:

(1) Korean copper coins (常平錢) are not to be used in trade.
(2) It is prohibited to trade in grain.
(3) Trade is permitted only on a barter system.
(4) Korea is concluding the treaty with Japan only and it is absolutely prohibited to bring any other foreign people to Korea.
(5) The introduction of opium and Western religion into Korea is prohibited.
(6) Shipwrecked sailors, adrift on the sea, are to be sent to their own country according to the old regulation under the *Kyorin* order. On the other hand, refugees disguised as persons adrift on the sea are to be identified and sent back to their own country.[4]

Accordingly Sin Hŏn insisted on inserting those six principles in the treaty. But the Japanese opposed Sin Hŏn's proposal on the pretext of insufficient time. Finally a compromise was reached as follows: the contents of Nos. 4 and 5 of the 'Six Principles' were henceforth to be inserted in a Japanese dispatch to Korea.[5]

---

4) WSIG, ISMJ; 26 January (lunar), Pyongja (1876); KJSDS, 1, p. 859; Tabohashi (1940), 1, pp. 479-480.
5) Tabohashi (1940), 1, pp. 492-494.

The Anti-Treaty Movement in Korea

It is easy to surmise that the Korean government encountered countless difficulties and opposition from many quarters regarding the treaty. As was already pointed out, the Taewŏngun's power was still prevalent and his political influence was immense in the court even after his resignation. He was a leader in the anti-treaty movement at the time.

On February 2, 1876, when Sin Hŏn conducted negotiations with Japan on Kanghwa Island, the Taewŏngun sent a letter to him through O Kyŏngsŏk and Hyŏn Sŏkun who went from Seoul to the island. In this letter, the Taewŏngun strongly opposed the conclusion of the treaty.[6]

Furthermore, on February 12, the Taewŏngun sent a letter full of threats to the Ministers who held a meeting in the State Council (議政府): it is lamentable to accept the Japanese *Sŏgye*, breaking the three hundred-year-old tradition. The Japanese gunboats and their costumes are all influenced by the Western powers and the Japanese came to Korea under Western control. The ulterior motive of the Japanese is to invade Korea with Western barbarians. The Japanese gunboats dared come into Korean internal waters and this very fact meant that the Japanese already knew that there were no faithful men in the Korean court. Finally, the Taewŏngun said that he himself, with his own followers,

---

6) *Simhaengilgi* (沁行日記, A Diary in Kangwha Island), 1, 8 January (lunar), Pyungja (1876), quoted from Tabohashi (1940), 1, p. 509.

would fight against Japanese invasion and die honorably. It was an obvious threat to all the people in the court.[7]

The Taewŏngun was not the only person who opposed the treaty. Innumerable Confucian scholars were strongly against the treaty and they were ready to fight to the last drop of their blood against it. Petitions to the throne were piled up and it was Ch'oi Ikhyŏn (崔益鉉) who triggered a movement against the treaty. On February 17, he carried an ax on his shoulder and submitted a famous petition to the throne.[8]

The Korean court was plunged into confusion and popular panic was widespread. It was the clash between the *Kyorin* order and the order of Western international law; the international political repercussions of this clash would be felt in Korean diplomatic history thereafter.

Dispatch of a Korean Envoy to Japan

After concluding the treaty, Sin Hŏn had an audience with King Kojong on March 1 (lunar February 6). King Kojong asked whether there was anything Sin Hŏn wanted to say in addition to his written report. In response Sin Hŏn emphasized the necessity of strengthening the military forces and said that if good relationships with China and Japan were kept, Korea could be protected from the intrusion of foreign powers. In addition, Sin

---

7) YHHN, 4, pp. 352-353.
8) SJWIG, 5, p. 504; ISN, 71, pp. 217-218; KJSL, 1, pp. 517-518.

Hŏn told the King about the importance of sending a goodwill mission to Japan as follows: Kuroda had asked for Korea to dispatch an envoy to Japan within six months of the conclusion of the treaty as a return courtesy. The Korean envoy could investigate Japanese customs and society. From Pusan, Sin Hŏn said that it would take seven or eight days to get to Japan by steamship. The King asked whether the envoy should be a Tongsinsa. Sin Hŏn deferentially responded that it was different from a traditional envoy in former times which had incurred too many expenses. The new envoy should simply be a person conversant in contemporary matters (解事者).[9]

Sin Hŏn's counsel reveals the undeniable significance of diplomatic history, because he inadvertently identified the transformation of the *Kyorin* order system itself.

According to the counsel of Sin Hŏn, the dispatch of a goodwill mission was decided. Japan was well aware that it was Sin Hŏn's efforts that were instrumental in deciding the problem of a mission to Japan. On February 17, 1877, Kuroda sent a letter of gratitude to Sin Hŏn and in March, Inoue also sent one.[10]

On March 17, 1876, Kim Kisu (金綺秀), having been promoted to the post of third minister of the Board of Rites (禮曹參議), became the first goodwill envoy to Japan after the Kanghwa Treaty. Hyŏn Sŏkun and Yi Yongsuk (李容肅), interpreters with the rank above upper-senior third grade, accompanied him. Members of this new mission numbered only around thirty men, whereas a retinue of a

---

9) SJWIG, 5, pp. 535-536; ISN, 71, pp. 246-249; KJSL, 1, p. 522.
10) YHHN, 4, p. 391, 392-393.

traditional Tongsinsa consisted of five hundred persons; this reduced number represented the business-like character of Kim Kisu's mission.

Kim Kisu left Pusan on May 22, 1876, and returned on June 28. His one-month visit to Japan was very important because he was the first official envoy to visit Japan since the Meiji Reformation and his opinions on the Meiji government could provide decisive information for future Korean policy towards Japan. Put another way, Kim Kisu was not a representative in the tradition of the *Kyorin* order, rather he was, in a sense, a diplomat under the Western international law system.

But unfortunately Kim Kisu was not the appropriate person to carry out this kind of historically significant mission. He was only a conservative Confucian scholar who refused to learn about new institutions from Japan. Therefore, Korea's selection of its first envoy was a great failure.

Kim Kisu had a farewell audience with the King on April 28 and he reported on his mission to the King on July 21.

At the farewell audience, King Kojong asked Kim Kisu several times to thoroughly observe and inspect the Japanese state of affairs, for it was the first time for the Korean government to dispatch an envoy to Meiji Japan.[11]

Examining his dialogues with King Kojong, it is clear that Kim Kisu did not meet the expectations of the King.

Kim Kisu did not follow the King's orders and moreover, he

---

11) SJWIG, 5, p. 605; ISN, 71, pp. 315-316; KJSL, 1, p. 525.

justified himself for not inspecting Japanese society. The Postscript (後敍) in his *Record of a Journey to Japan* (日東記游) is the very writing of his justification of his conduct. In this article, he claimed that it was not an envoy's main duty to inspect another country's situation, for such inspection was nothing but a trivial and minor task.[12]

On that day, the King said that Kim might stay in Japan for fifteen days, which was the official duration of a stay in Japan under the *Kyorin* order, but he was not obliged to strictly observe that duty. He could stay longer, if he so desired. However, he refused the entire schedule of inspections arranged by the Japanese, on the pretext that he was not allowed to stay in Japan longer than fifteen days. We can find many such instances in his *Record*.

After his return to Korea, Kim had an audience with King Kojong. The King asked various questions about international politics, Japanese domestic politics, cultural affairs and about the military forces in Japan, but Kim could not adequately answer those questions. He was a man far from the King's expectations. Let us look more closely at part of the dialogue between King Kojong and Kim:

> King: Besides the *Special Report on Facts Heard and Seen* (聞見別 單),[13] is there anything more that you want to tell me?
> Kisu: There is nothing to say besides what there is in the report.[14]

---

12) ITKY, p. 111.
13) TMHG, 4, pp. 4176-4179; ITKY, pp. 105-110.
14) ITKY, p. 129.

King: I hear that Japan is trading with various other countries and did you see or meet any foreigners staying in Japan?

Kisu: No, I didn't. The foreigners look more or less the same and it was very difficult to distinguish them from one another.[15]

King: Are there scholars specializing on Western countries (洋學者) in Japan?

Kisu: I am not sure that the discipline of 'Western learning (洋學)' exists in Japan.

King: Did you ever see any matches?[16]

Kisu: No, I have never seen such a thing. I did not ask for them, because I could not learn how to use them even if I saw them.[17]

King: After the Japanese people had contacted our country, what was their opinion of our country?

Kisu: I have not yet heard of anything about their opinions.

King: [After hearing from Kim that England is the most powerful country in the world] Then, besides England, what about other countries?

Kisu: I am ignorant about other countries.[18]

King: Are their rifles long or short in length? Are they the same size as their pistols (六穴銃)?

Kisu: I have never seen any pistols.[19]

Besides the insufficiency of his knowledge, he did not mention a very important Russian question, as will be explained later.

---

15) Ibid, p. 130.

16) Koreans at that time made fire using flints. The King was aware that matches were used in Japan and was curious about them.

17) Ibid, p. 131.

18) Ibid, p. 132.

19) Ibid, p. 133.

In his *Record of a Journey to Japan*, Kim wrote that Moriyama and Miyamoto criticized the dilatory Korean attitude in negotiations and the evasion of responsibility by the Korean officials. They also claimed that their Korean counterparts should change their attitude to negotiation. Even though this was an important aspect of Japanese views regarding Korea, Kim could not answer the King's questions.

In spite of Kim's inadequate and ignorant answers, there were a few interesting dialogues between the two. Let us look at an example:

> King: Russia [魯西亞, a new pronunciation of Russia], what is Russia?
> Kisu: That is Arasa [俄羅斯, a Korean pronunciation of Russia which was used before].
> King: Then, why do people say Russia for Arasa?
> Kisu: Russia is another name for Arasa.
> King: In the *Yinghuan chiluel* (瀛環志略) or *Haikuo tuchi* (海國圖志), do they use the term Russia?
> Kisu: That is correct.[20]
> King: Which country is the most talented (and competent) country in the Western world?
> Kisu: It is England.
> King: Where is America?
> Kisu: It is situated on the western part of the West and the eastern part of the East.[21]

We need to pay special attention to Kim's report that England

---

20) Ibid, p. 130.
21) Ibid, p. 132.

was the most developed country in the world. Pak Kyusu, from the time of the *General Sherman* Incident in 1866, perceived America as the most equitable country without any ambition of territorial aggrandizement.[22] It is well-known fact that King Kojong was very interested in America.

But a new realization that Great Britain was the most powerful state began to circulate among Korean intellectuals, as seen in Kim's report. Yi Tongin's (李東仁) connection with the British embassy in Tokyo in 1880 does not seem to have been a mere chance-encounter. The historically important relationship between Yi Tongin, the secret envoy of King Kojong, and E. Satow, the Secretary of the British Embassy, will be clarified in my forthcoming book, *Korea and the Dissolution of the Sadae Order.* Another notable thing is that it was around this time that King Kojong heard the new pronunciation of Russia for the first time.

Concerning the first Korean envoy to Japan, the basic Japanese stance should be noted. As already mentioned, dispatching Kim Kisu to Japan came to be realized by the strong assertion of Kuroda and Inoue, as well as by the counsel of Sin Hŏn. Japan seized this opportunity to show Kim a developed Japan. By doing this, the Japanese government hoped to make Korea dependent upon Japan. Moriyama's advocacy of an alliance among the three far eastern countries[23] started from this stream of the Japanese intentions.

Before Kim Kisu's arrival, the Japanese Ministry of Foreign

---

22) Yongkoo Kim (2001), pp. 82-90.
23) Ibid, p. 3.

Affairs had prepared a complex and thorough inspection schedule for Kim, who was to go on a tour of inspection of the ministries of the Army and Navy, and inspect all the systems in each ministry. Kim also was supposed to visit various parks and factories, where he could learn about their technological innovations, in order to broaden his views.[24] But Kim refused almost all of these Japanese proposals and he actually visited only a few places.

Nevertheless, the purpose which Japan set for the Korean envoy was achieved to some degree. Kim was astonished by the fact that the whole country was striving for measures to 'enrich the nation and strengthen the army (富國强兵)' and Kim was also startled to see Japanese society so developed and Westernized.

Kim Kisu's sheer astonishment was aptly captured in various instances in his *Record of a Journey to Japan*, and especially in his *Special Report on Facts Heard and Seen*.

Yi Yongsuk who accompanied Kim also reported in his *Special Report on Facts Heard and Seen*,[25] where he noted that Japan possessed a strong army of some 600,000 or 700,000 soldiers.

But Kim insisted that Korea should not blindly follow the Japanese argument about the 'enrichment of the nation and strengthening of the army.' He defined such argument as commercial relations and claimed that it could be only obtained by engaging in international trade. Many countries came to Japan for trade and Japan was the only country that went abroad for trade. Consequently, prices would inevitably begin to rise and resources

---

24) Tabohashi, 1, pp. 574-575.
25) TMHG, 4, p. 4179.

would grow scarce; this so-called art could not be a long term policy for Korea.[26]

But after visiting Japan, Kim Kisu's prior opinions regarding Japan changed considerably. He was extremely impressed by the fact that most people in Japan were hard workers, kind and friendly, and that it was very clean everywhere. Kim was also surprised to see that there were no beggars or handicapped people on the streets. Yi Yongsuk, who frequented China for a long time, shared the same opinion with Kim about this aspect of Japanese society.[27]

The Emergence of Russian Question in the Far East

One of the most significant political results of dispatching the first envoy to Japan was that Korea began to be absorbed into the British sphere of international propaganda when Great Britain and Russia confronted each other in the world arena. Geographically, Japan was in a good position to resist Russian expansion towards the south. In this regard, Japan and England shared the same basic international political stance.

The Russian matter started to be mentioned from the first encounter between the Meiji government and Korea on Kanghwa Island in 1876. On February 15, 1876, the Japanese translators, Urase Hiroshi (浦懶裕) and Arakawa Tokushi (荒川德滋) came to

---

26) TMHK, 4, p. 4179; ITKY, pp. 109-110.
27) ITKY, pp. 61-62.

meet O Kyŏngsŏk and in this meeting Sin Hŏn asked which was the most powerful country in the world at that time. They answered that it was Russia and that every country was afraid of her.[28]

Inoue told Kim Kisu that he himself had told the Korean delegates about the Russian threat earlier at the meeting on Kanghwa Island. Kim Kisu met Councilor Inoue Kaoru for the first time at the banquet for the Korean envoy on June 3, 1876, and afterwards they met several more times.

On the afternoon of June 4, Inoue visited Kim and on June 8, Inoue hosted a banquet in his house for Kim. In this meeting Inoue emphasized the threat of Russia and tried to make Kim understand the international situation in the Far Eastern world. Let us look at what Inoue said about Russia.

> I mentioned several times at the meeting on Kanghwa that there was every indication of the Russian army's movement towards the south. Whenever our people go to Russia, they find that Russians are making heavy military weapons and stockpiling military provisions in the regions around the Hei Long (黑龍) River. What do you think their intention is in the future? I esteem it necessary for Korea to repair her guns and train soldiers in order to protect herself from a Russian invasion.[29]

Inoue also showed Kim Kisu a world map, in order to indicate the geographical fact that Korea and Russia were situated so close

---

28) *Simhaeilgi*, book 1, quoted from Tabohashi, 1, p. 494.
29) ITKY, p. 51, 122.

together on the map. After being a little inebriated, he laid stress again on the importance of the Russian matter as follows.

Do you remember what I said last time? I told you many times that Russia is interested in Korea. I am not a paralytic who has had a mental breakdown. And if I had no conviction about what I said, why should I say such things. When you go back to Korea, please let the Korean court know the danger posed by Russia and prepare for it. [Then he brought out a world map] I am giving this map to you and I hope that you will look at this map from time to time. The distance of each degree is indicated on the map. Thereby you can judge the distance between your country and Russia.[30]

After this meeting with Kim Kisu, Inoue continued his anti-Russian argument. He sent a letter to Sin Hŏn in March 1877. At the beginning of the letter, Inoue wrote that while Kim Kisu might have reported to the Korean court everything that he had seen and experienced in Japan, Inoue himself was not entirely free from anxiety over Russia. Considering the world situation, Inoue wrote that he could not remain silent about the future of Korea. Because there existed an enormous dragon in the north, whose energy was ceaselessly increasing, and it would swallow whatever there was in the world. Furthermore, he asserted that Korea should ally itself with as many countries as possible in order to maintain the balance of power in world politics lest she should be isolated from the world. Thereby he advised Kim Kisu to commence sending Korean students to Japan in order to learn the

---

30) Ibid, p. 52, 123.

situation of various countries.[31]

Nevertheless Kim Kisu did not report the important Russian question to King Kojong. Notwithstanding his ignorance of the world situation, his visit to Japan had some positive effects on Korea's perceptions of new international circumstances. In his writing, he compared the essence of Western international law with the balance of power system in the period of Spring and Autumn.[32] He might have heard about *Wankuo kongfa* (萬國公法) while staying in Japan, or might have read at least the preface of Zhang Sigui (張斯桂) in the *Wankuo kongfa*.

Zhang, in his preface, compared the contemporary world powers with those in the period of Spring and Autumn (春秋) and of the Warring States (戰國). America was, through a metaphor, compared to Qin (秦), Russia to Chu (楚), England and France to Qi (齊), Austria and Prussia to Lu (魯) and Wei (衛), Turkey to Song (宋) and Italy to Zheng (鄭). He explained that the coexistence of these countries was possible because of the observance of treaties concluded between them.[33]

Furthermore Kim Kisu came to know something about 'full power (全權)', an important concept in Western international law. He wrote as follows.

There are terminologies like 'ambassador plenipotentiary' and

31) YHHN, 4, pp. 392-393.
32) ITKY, p. 70.
33) For *Wankuo kungfa*, see my works indicated in the Bibliography.

'minister plenipotentiary.' Once he received an order from the king, he could do whatever he wants to do in order to achieve profits for his country. In such matters as fall under his jurisdiction, he is allowed to do anything at will. He can kill or free anybody, and he can make matters to be delayed or hastened, as he wishes. Therefore this is called 'full power.'[34]

Nevertheless, as already mentioned, Kim Kisu's role as an envoy to Japan ended in failure.

Permanent Residence of the Japanese Envoy in Seoul

The Japanese government decided to send Miyamoto Koichi (宮本小一) to Seoul in order to discuss the succeeding problems arising from the Kanghwa Treaty. For that matter, it had asked Kim Kisu several times that future negotiations in Seoul be conducted smoothly without delays or unnecessary arguing.

The day after Kim Kisu's report of his mission, the Korean court appointed Cho Inhŭi (趙寅熙), Second Minister of the Board of Punishments (刑曹參判), as a treaty negotiator (講修官) and Yi Yongsuk as a temporary translator (差備譯官). Myamoto, who stayed in Seoul from July 30 to August 26, held formal meetings with Cho Inhŭi twelve times and had one special conference with Sin Hŏn and Yun Chasŭng. The Additional Articles Appended to the Kanghwa Treaty and the Trade Regulations were thereby

---

34) ITKY, p. 70.

signed on August 24, 1876. But it was not possible to settle the permanent stationing of envoys in either capital city.

The conflict between the systems of permanent envoys in Western international law and the system of Tongsinsa under the *Kyorin* order was explained in Chapter 4, as were the difficult negotiations arising from this clash. Myamoto could not easily solve this acute issue. Since the Japanese interpreted Article II as the establishment of a permanent envoy system, Myamoto proposed that an official residence of envoys might be lent or newly built.[35]

Cho Inhŭi strongly opposed Myamoto's proposal. His main argument went as follows: if a Japanese embassy were to be opened in Seoul, unexpected things would necessarily arise between the two countries. Since there would not be other diplomatic officers residing in Seoul, a Japanese envoy would not have anything to do in Korea for diplomatic activities. The Japanese envoy in Seoul could not make contact with Japanese offices in treaty ports, since these were too remote to be reached easily. If something routine happens between the two countries, it would be enough to correspond by the *Sŏgye*. And if something grave occurred, a temporary envoy would be dispatched to either capital city. Therefore Korea could not assent to the establishment of a Japanese embassy in Seoul.[36]

Faced with such a strong opposition, Myamoto requested a direct meeting with Sin Hŏn, the very person who had signed the

---

35) NGB, 9, doc. no. 66, p. 211.
36) WSIG, ISMJ, June 18 (lunar), 1876.

Treaty of Kanghwa, in order to clearly understand the Korean position in this matter.

Therefore Sin Hŏn and Yun Chasŭng, the former Korean delegates to the Kanghwa treaty negotiations, went to Myamoto's residence near the West Gate (西大門) on August 13.

On this occasion, Sin Hŏn made the Korean viewpoints very clear as follows.

> Our country has never violated any regulation in the Treaty of Kanghwa. As stipulated in Article II, we understand that persons such as your representatives (理事官) would reside in Seoul. But there are no treaty regulations about the establishment of an embassy. Our government would never consent to the matter which is not stipulated in the treaty. The stipulation in Article II that "the Japanese representative shall be free at all times to remain in Korea or to return to Japan at will" means that Korea would not urge him to leave for Japan.[37]

After hearing Sin Hŏn's explanation, Miyamoto could not help but drop the issue. The subsidiary arguments, concerning whether the families of a minister were to come or not, were naturally dropped also.

Far from resolving the problem of a permanent residence for Japanese ministers in Seoul, Myamoto complicated the issue still further before he left Korea. On the day of signing of the Trade Regulations, Myamoto, according to Cho Inhŭi's request, handed the latter a diplomatic note. In this note, Myamoto clarified that the

---

37) NGB, 9, doc. no. 85, p. 256.

purpose of the residence of a Japanese minister in Seoul was to conduct affairs of mutual intercourse and that Japanese officials in the treaty ports would take charge of trade affairs. Myamoto also conceded that the route to Seoul was to be fixed.[38] This note was contrary to the intention of the Japanese government and it also left Japan in an unfavorable and vulnerable position. The Korean government understood, on account of this note, that Japan withdrew the issue of ministers being stationed in Seoul. As this problem was pending, the negotiating route between Korea and Japan was, like the route under the *Kyorin* order, from the Japanese consul in Pusan to the Korean prefects of Tongrae Prefecture to the Korean court in Seoul.[39]

---

38) KHOM, Japanese Documents, 1, doc. no. 10, p. 8; NGB, 9, doc. no. 99. pp. 294-296.

39) The resolution of all these problems had to wait until Kim Hongjip (金弘集) visited Japan in 1880 and the Korean court adopted a new foreign policy. For Kim's epoch-making visit to Japan, see my forthcoming book, *Korea and the Dissolution of the Sadae Order.*

Having been promoted to the position of Minister Resident, Hanabusa Yoshimoto (花房義質) arrived in Seoul on December 17, 1880. On December 27, he had an audience with King Kojong and presented the Japanese sovereign's message. Afterwards the Korean government tacitly recognized the residence of the Japanese envoys in Seoul. The problem of the stationing of the envoy's family members was finally resolved after the Imo military uprising of 1882 (壬午軍亂).

Tariff-Free Trade

The Trade Regulations stipulating procedures for import and export to and from Korea was also signed on August 24, 1876. Its major contents were the prohibition of opium sales, the import and export of grains in the treaty ports, and the exemption of port duties for government-owned Japanese ships.

But along with the conclusion of these regulations, Myamoto handed Cho Inhǔi a very important note, the contents of which Cho unwarily accepted. The gist of Myamoto's note ran as follows.

> Our customs house shall not levy any duties on the export of goods to your country and shall also not levy any duties on Korean goods imported by Japanese people into our internal territory in years to come. Our government has secretly decided on this utmost generous and lenient policy.[40]

Such Japanese logic is a manifest deception, apparent to anyone who has even a little knowledge of international trade. Tariff duty exemption inevitably leads to the detriment of the weaker country. Anticipating possible Korean opposition against the Japanese proposal for the exemption of duties, the Japanese government had instructed Myamoto to allow a 5% ad valorem duty for import and export goods if necessary.[41]

---

40) NGB, 9, enclosure 3 of doc. no. 92, p. 284.
41) NGB, 9, doc. no. 73, p. 220.

But Cho Inhŭi sent a dispatch to Myamoto replying that Korea would also exempt import and export goods from taxation for several years to come.[42]

It can be surmised from this that the Korean court did not yet fully grasp the importance of customs duties. So began a period of trade without tariffs until the end of the 1870s.

---

42) ISMJ, July 6 (lunar), 1876.

6

The Dissolution of the *Kyorin* Order and the Role of the World Powers

___ China

___ Great Britain

___ Russia

___ The United States

___ France and Germany

The Kanghwa Treaty led inevitably to the dissolution of the Kyorin *order and in that sense it was a watershed event in Far Eastern international history. It is, therefore, an important academic task to investigate how the world powers perceived and interpreted that treaty. China sought to maintain Korea as a* 'waifan' *even in the changed international system. Great Britain, the leading world power, tried to manipulate the changing Korean situation in order to restrain Russian expansion in the Far East. The British Ministry of the Navy already planned the occupation of Port Hamilton, while Russia, due to her economic underdevelopment, had to continue her traditional 'waiting policy' toward the Korean peninsula. Meanwhile, the United States had not yet awakened from its nightmare of 1871.*[1]

---

1) For the U.S. invasion of Korea in 1871, see Yongkoo Kim (2001), pp. 97-121.

China

The Zongli Yamen already decided its basic position toward the Korean question on January 17, 1876, as follows: Although Korea was a vassal-state, she was autonomous in 'government exhortations and restrictions (政教禁令).' Therefore Korea should conclude a treaty with Japan independently.[2]

Accordingly, the Chinese Board of Rites notified Korea of the Zongli Yamen's ruling, along with all the diplomatic proceedings with Japan relating to the suzerainty problem. Korea received these documents on February 5, while Yun Chasŭng and Moriyama met for preliminary negotiations on Kanghwa Island.

Two days after the Zongli Yamen decided on the general lines of its Korean policy, Li Hungchang expressed his concrete viewpoints to the Yamen. The gist of his ideas are as follows: Korea, being weak, cannot be a match for Japan. If Korea counted on Chinese protection and asked China for help according to the precedent in the Ming dynasty (明朝), how could China deal with this matter? If Japan decided to invade Korea, how could China prevent the war? If Japan invades Korea, Manchuria would be in danger and its future trouble would be beyond description. Japan, of course, insists that she is seeking peace with Korea and would not use its armed forces indiscriminately. The truth or falsehood of this statement aside, the moment has come to start planning for

---

2) ZRJS, 1, doc. no. 1, p. 1.

the future. China must hastily send Korea a letter of counsel that Korea must put aside its ill-feeling towards Japan and extend every courtesy to that nation in order to forestall trouble. Li concluded that China would not directly intervene in the Korean-Japanese negotiations and that Korea should finally accept China's advice.[3]

The Zongli Yamen completely agreed with Li's opinion.[4] However such Chinese advice was, in fact, a kind of threat to Korea.

At this juncture, Li Hungchang managed to find a channel for negotiating with Yi Yuwŏn (李裕元), a leading figure in Korean political circles at that time. With this connection, Li could assert pressure on the Korean court.

Yi Yuwŏn, the First Minister of the Office of Ministers-without-Portfolio (領中樞府使), went to Peking in the summer of 1875 in order to request a patent of appointment for the Korean Crown Prince. During his stay in China, Yi sent a letter to Li Hungchang. Li received this letter on January 9, 1876 and he promptly replied to Yi the next day.

Yi's letter was an ordinary one, written out of courtesy, inquiring after Li's health. But Li's return letter, though a short one, presented distinct political implications. Li, comparing the present situation of Korea to that of China's past, emphasized the necessity of concluding a treaty with Japan.[5]

King Kojong also read Li's letter and was undoubtedly

---

3) LGCC, 5, pp. 104-106.
4) ZRJS, 1, doc. no. 2, p. 2.
5) LGCC, 5, p. 105.

encouraged to pursue his new Japanese policy. Yi Yuwon and Li Hungchang thereafter exchanged 17 letters altogether; this private connection between two such influential politicians had a considerable impact on contemporary Korean politics.[6]

There was another channel through which China exerted her influence over Korea. At that time, Zheng Jishi (鄭基世), the Chinese imperial envoy, arrived in Korea to inform of a patent of appointment of the Crown Prince. King Kojong met him at Mohwa Kwan (慕華館, Commemoration House for the Chinese) outside the West Gate (西大門), Seoul, on February 16 and asked him whether he knew about the arrival of a Japanese ship in Korea. Zheng replied that he had heard about it while he was on his way to Korea. He added that he knew that the Zongli Yamen had sent Korea its advice not to jeopardize peace and harmony with Japan and to conduct negotiations over a conclusion of a treaty with her.[7]

The Chinese Board of Rites, the Zongli Yamen, the Superintendent for the Northern Ports, and the Imperial Envoy all strongly advised the Korean court to establish treaty relations with Japan. Amid the conservative atmosphere in the whole nation, King Kojong and his followers were strongly encouraged by such Chinese support in their efforts to pursue a conciliatory policy toward Japan.

---

6) Yongkoo Kim (1997), pp. 193-198; Harada (1997), pp. 192-204.
7) SJWIG, 5, p. 504.

Great Britain

Great Britain, of course, was the most powerful country in the world during those years. As such, England showed her deep political concerns regarding the Korean matter and she also thoroughly analyzed what to do to best profit from the conflict between Korea and Japan. One of the noteworthy political and military deliberations was the plan, made as early as July 1875, to occupy Port Hamilton (Kŏmundo, 巨文島), three small islands off Korea's southern coast. It is a well-known fact that in April 1885 Great Britain occupied those islands and that British soldiers stayed there for two years. However it is remarkable that the occupation of Port Hamilton had been discussed by English officials ten years before the actual military operations took place.

The first Japanese diplomatic démarche relating to the Korean problem, according to *NGB*, which is the basic collection of Japanese diplomatic documents, was the announcement of the *Unyo* Incident to the foreign envoys residing in Tokyo on October 3, 1875.[8] But in the Records in the Ministry of Foreign Affairs (外務省記錄), unpublished documents kept in the Japanese Foreign Ministry Archives (外交史料館), we can find related materials before that Japanese official announcement regarding several meetings between H. Parkes, the English Minister to Japan, and Terashima Munenori (寺島宗則), the Minister of the Japanese Ministry of

---

8) NGB, 8, doc. no. 52, p. 121.

Foreign Affairs.[9] Also in the English documents, we can find that Parkes kept a watchful eye on diplomatic negotiations between Korea and Japan especially after 1873.[10]

The British government also received information on Korea from its embassy in Peking. W. S. F. Mayers, a British embassy secretary, who was very fluent in Chinese and also, at the same time, managed to communicate in Korean, met twice with the Korean translators who accompanied the envoys to China, on February 16, 1875 and on December 26, 1875. Through these Korean translators, Mayers gathered information about the Korean-Japanese negotiations.[11]

On July 17, 1875, H. Parkes sent a general report to London concerning the growing tensions between Korea and Japan.[12] Subsequently on July 20, he delivered two important documents to E. S. Derby, the Secretary of State for Foreign Affairs. One was a telegram[13] and the other was a secret and confidential long letter,[14] which Derby received on July 23 and on September 13 respectively. As these were the first British materials discussing the occupation of Port Hamilton, it is essential to examine them closely.

The relevant part of Parkes' telegram ran as follows.

---

9) HISC, 1, pp. 1-40.
10) Plunkett to Derby, Dec. 13, 1875, AADM, p. 7.
11) Jones (1936), pp. 104-106; Coates (1988), p. 352.
12) Parkes to Derby, July 17, 1875, BDFA, Part I, Series E, Vol. 2, pp. 41-42.
13) Parkes to Derby, July 20, 1875, BDFA, I-E-2, p. 39.
14) Parkes to Derby, July 20, 1875, BDFA, I-E-2, pp. 42-44.

An understanding of Russia and Japan as to (an) attack on Korea is reported. A large German corvette is also surveying the west coast, with a view, as it is believed, to occupation .... In view of highly probable eventualities, I also advise, with (the) Admiral's concurrence, that we should immediately occupy Port Hamilton, if this has not already been done by another power .... The great importance of these islands is well known to Admiral Shadwell.

H. Parkes explained in detail the political reason for the occupation in his long letter, another document which he sent on July 20. The following is the gist of the report.

(R)eports reach us by way of the United States that Russia herself intends to attack Korea .... I imagine that little argument is needed to support the general belief that Russia wishes to advance south along the Korean Peninsula as soon as she sees that a convenient time for doing so has arrived .... It is easy to see how Japan and Russia could play into each other's hands in the case of both being willing, either separately or combined, to engage in operations against Korea.

The plan of a joint occupation of that country might be looked forward to as promising even greater advantages to Russia than those which she has derived from the joint occupation of Sakhalin. The desire of the German government to obtain a footing in these regions has also long been a subject of common report. A new corvette has just arrived on the station and her first movement is to proceed to the west coast of Korea for the purpose, as is alleged, of surveying, but, as is commonly believed, of finding some position among the numerous islands off that coast that would be suited to German requirements.

Under these circumstances, I venture to recommend that we

should undertake the survey of the south coast of Korea, and that the small group of islands known as Port Hamilton should be occupied by ourselves before a position of such great importance passes into the hands of another power. [Port Hamilton] commands the China, Japan and Yellow Seas, and its importance as a military position, and as a depôt for coal and stores, in any contest that we might have with Russia, with China, with Japan, or with any other maritime power, is too obvious to need remark (sic). If the occupation of Port Hamilton, therefore, had no other result than to lead the Korean government to negotiate with us, and to accept friendly intercourse, the step would prove of great value to our future interests.

Vice-Admiral A. P. Ryder, the Commander in Chief, China Fleet, totally agreed with the opinion of H. Parkes and sent a telegram and a long letter of the occupation plan to the Secretary to the Admiralty on July 20. The latter document explains the necessity of the occupation point by point. His descriptions were very precise and detailed as he was a naval strategist. The core of his letter ran as follows.

(1) Sir Harry Parkes has sent a somewhat similar report to the Foreign Office. The subjects alluded to are as follows: (a) The Russians have lately acquired Sakhalin, have moved from the Amur to Vladivostok, and are believed to be making preparations to annex Korea. (b) The German government, who, Mr. Wade informed me, was coveting the same island for headquarters in these seas, has sent the *Ariadne*, a large corvette, to survey on (sic) the west coast of Korea. (c) The Japanese have sent a vessel to survey on (sic) the east coast of Korea, and are believed to be

acting in concert with Russia. (d) The islands off the south coast are in the track of our merchant vessels from Japan to Chefoo (芝罘), and the Koreans have massacred the wrecked crews of numerous vessels.

(2) Under these circumstances, I am of opinion, and Sir Harry Parkes concurs with me: (a) That Her Majesty's ship *Sylvia* might be more usefully employed in surveying the southwest coast of Korea than in the inland sea, with her headquarters at Port Hamilton. (b) That it would be of great advantage to English interests in these seas in the future if we occupied Port Hamilton permanently.

(3) The Koreans are an uncivilized race, who massacre the crews of wrecked merchant-vessels, who refuse to have any intercourse with foreigners. This being the case, I hold that we stand upon no ceremony with them as to taking possession of an island lying twenty miles off their coast.

(4) I can hardly over-estimate the great importance of our having some possession in these seas which we can call our own. A dockyard, so called, at Shanghai, stores at Yokohama on foreign ground, are little or no use in war. In war with China, or Japan, or Russia, or any other nation, it would be of the utmost importance to us to have some *point d'appui*, where would be our coal depôt, our stores, our hospital, our dock. It should be sufficiently far south not to be frozen up in winter; it should be within easy reach of China, Japan, Russia; it should be easy of defence, have a secure harbour. All these qualifications are united in Port Hamilton, and the last words uttered to me by Sir Charles Shadwell were: "Don't lose sight of the great importance of our possessing Port Hamilton.[15)]

---

15) Ryder to the Secretary of Admiralty, July 20, 1875, BDFA, I-E-2, pp. 45-46.

I quote Ryder's letter here in detail, because his military logic had a vitality even after ten years, in 1885, when the Board of Admiralty actually ordered the occupation of Port Hamilton.

When the British Foreign Office received Parkes' telegram on July 23, it was very critical of Parkes' opinion. But its critique was not based on the occupation itself, but on its timing. The next day the Foreign Office sought the opinion of the Board of Admiralty as to Port Hamilton. On July 26, the latter department sent the former its opinion as follows: (1) the subject appears to be for the consideration of the government. (2) If Her Majesty's naval forces take possession of Port Hamilton, questions would no doubt arise as to the right of Great Britain. (3) The Board, however, is ready to send any telegraphic instructions to the naval Commander-in-Chief on the Chinese station.[16]

The Foreign Office also instructed the embassies in Berlin and Saint Petersburg to investigate the attitudes of the governments concerned as to the Korean peninsula. The embassies replied that German and Russian postures in the Far East were quite contrary to those described in Parkes' reports.[17]

Consequently, the government finally decided not to occupy Port Hamilton, as the British takeover of the island would, no doubt, encourage other powers to take similar action in the region. Ultimately, in the year 1875, the British were not in such an acute military confrontation with Russia to forcefully seize such an isolated island as Port Hamilton.

---

16) The Secretary of Admiralty to Bourke, July 26, BDFA, I-E-2, pp. 40-41.
17) Jones (1936), pp. 112-113.

E. S. Derby therefore dispatched two telegrams to H. Parkes, one on August 3 and the other the next day, instructing that "Her Majesty's government do (sic) not think it desirable to set to other nations the example of occupying places to which Great Britain has no title."[18]

On August 24, H. Parkes sent a long dispatch to the Earl of Derby that he would follow these instructions, and he frankly admitted that his judgment concerning the occupation of Port Hamilton was based on false information i.e., that Japan would soon provoke war with Korea and many Russians were staying in Tsushima.[19]

Parkes also enclosed a report of a field trip completed by F. R. Plunkett, the secretary at the British embassy in Tokyo. Plunkett and his suite visited Port Hamilton for three days, on August 4~6, 1875, and conducted thorough field work.

Plunkett and his people directly communicated with the Koreans, which would make this the first encounter between the two peoples. Subsequently, they visited Tsushima; afterwards, they went to Pusan, on August 9. They invited Moriyama Shigeru, who had been staying in Pusan, to climb aboard the British ship, in order to find out the actual status of the ongoing negotiations between Korea and Japan. Plunkett reported to H. Parkes that his geographical information about Port Hamilton solely relied on the imperfect map of E. Belcher, which had been made thirty years earlier. He also informed H. Parkes that there were no Russians

---

18) Derby to Parkes, Aug. 3 & 4, 1875, BDFA, I-E-2, p. 41.
19) Parkes to Derby, Aug. 24, 1875, BDFA, I-E-2, p. 46.

living in Tsushima.[20]

Thus, the episode of the planned occupation of Port Hamilton ended and did not come to fruition in 1875. Professor G. Daniel, a specialist on Parkes' diplomatic life in Japan, reached the conclusion that "from this point on his attitudes towards Korea became strangely emotional and unstable." "This change," Daniel presumed, "may have resulted from his declining health or perhaps his exaggerated fears of Russia."[21]

In 1875, submarine cables were already in place between England and Japan, allowing Parkes' plan in Tokyo to be immediately known to the British government in London, while the latter could quickly cope with the matter in the Far East. This situation was strikingly different from that in 1866, when France invaded Korea. At that time, no submarine cables had been laid between the European continent and the Far East, a fact which gave French diplomats and admirals vast discretionary powers.

Notwithstanding all of these refusals from the government, Parkes persistently clung to the idea that England might be the first nation in the world to conclude a treaty with Korea. In the late summer of 1875, there occurred an incident whereby a drifting Korean sailor was rescued by an English ship along the Japanese shore. Parkes wanted to hand over this man to Korea and to take this opportunity for opening negotiations with Korea.

Parkes requested permission from the British government to visit

---

20) Plunkett to Parkes, Aug. 11, 1875, BDFA, I-E-2, pp. 48-53.
21) Daniels (1996), p. 159.

Korea, but he was again refused permission to do so. The British government worried that if Parkes were allowed to conduct negotiations to conclude a treaty with Korea, as M. C. Perry had done with Japan in 1854, it might cause an unwanted war in the Korean peninsula. The British Foreign Office simply ordered that the shipwrecked sailor should be sent to Pusan through Japanese authorities.[22]

But H. Parkes did not give up on his idea of concluding a treaty with Korea. He defended his position regarding Korea with the rationale of a possible Russian encroachment into this region. Too sensitive of the Russian threat, he somewhat exaggerated Russian power in the Far East, repeatedly sending his government reports concerning Russian policy. The Foreign Office in London, however, was indifferent to Parkes' opinion. His long letter to the Earl of Derby on December 31, 1875 clearly reveals Parkes' attitude towards the Russian threat. The contents of this letter can be paraphrased as follows.

Wonsan (元山) and Pusan could be occupied and held with the utmost ease with the forces that Russia had in Eastern Siberia and Sakhalin. If Russia obtains possession of Pusan, or any other equally commanding place in Korea, she would be able to control the whole of the foreign trade of China and Japan. H. Parkes strongly suspected the existence of an understanding on the Korean question, which was concluded as early as the previous July, between Russia and Japan. With such an alliance Japan

---

22) Parkes to Derby, Dec. 6, 1875, Daniels (1996), pp. 161-162.

hoped that she would be able to ensure success, either in negotiations, or in war. On the other hand, Russia would render Japan material service and would establish a claim to territorial compensation. Therefore, the British government should give due attention to this important Korean question.[23]

H. Parkes continuously advised his government that England should take measures to deal with the Russian threat, until it was reported that Korea and Japan had concluded the Kanghwa Treaty. His real intention was not expressed clearly in his reports, but it could be surmised that he supported active British involvement, such as a possible occupation of strategic places like Port Hamilton.[24] Furthermore, he might be suspected of having aimed to provoke a conflict between Korea and Japan. Japanese newspapers strongly criticized him for reportedly instigating bellicose people in Japan to open hostilities toward Korea.[25]

When the Kanghwa Treaty was finally concluded, Parkes again pleaded with his government once more to conduct negotiations with Korea, but his proposal was again refused.[26]

However, the British embassy in Tokyo continuously requested the Japanese Ministry of Foreign Affairs for information about the Korean attitude toward the world powers during the meeting on Kanghwa Island. H. Parkes was simply told that Korea never mentioned the Western powers and had also asked Japan not to

23) Parkes to Derby, Dec. 31, 1875, AADM, pp. 16-17.
24) Parkes to Derby, Jan. 10, 1876, AADM, p. 31, 33-34.
25) Plunkett to Derby, Dec. 9, 1875, AADM, p. 5.
26) Daniels (1996), p. 163.

bring foreigners to Korea in the future. Nevertheless, on March 3, 1876, in the middle of the meeting with Terashima, the Minister of Foreign Affairs, Parkes obtained the information that Korea also foresaw contact with the Western countries. Terashima gave Parkes as an evidence that a Korean high official who had visited China told the Japanese delegates that once the treaty with Japan was concluded, Korea might go on to establish relations with other countries.[27] On March 26, Moriyama who had participated in concluding the Kanghwa Treaty, visited Parkes and told him that Korea was actually arranging negotiations with other countries.[28]

Russia

The Japanese government contacted Russia in order to get information about her attitude in the event that Japan took military action against Korea in the future. Parkes' suspicion of the existence of a Russo-Japanese agreement was therefore not totally groundless.

E. K. Byutsov, the Russian minister to Japan, sent a report on the Korean question to A. M. Gorchakov, the Minister of Foreign Affairs, on August 22, 1873. According to this document, Soejima Taneomi (副島種臣), the Japanese Foreign Minister, reportedly asked for Russian neutrality in the event that Japan despatched

---

27) Parkes to Derby, Mar. 3, 1876, AADM, p. 42.
28) Parkes to Derby, Mar. 27, 1876, AADM, p. 47. For the conference between Parkes and Moriyama, see Yongkoo Kim (2001), pp. 235-236.

50,000 soldiers to Korea. Byutsov in his turn asked what Japan would do in Korea after the military action. Soejima avoided giving any definite answer.[29]

At the end of August, Soejima again met with Byutsov and requested Russian cooperation for the passage of Japanese soldiers to Korea along the Russian coast. But Byutsov declined to answer with the excuse that he had not received any instruction on this matter.

On October 8, 1873, the Russian Foreign Ministry instructed Byutsov to notify the Japanese government that if Japanese soldiers landed in Russian territory, the world powers would suspect the existence of a secret agreement between Russia and Japan.[30] This instruction amounted to a Russian refusal of the Japanese proposal. The Japanese government sought Russian acquiescence in the passage of Japanese troops in return for the Japanese surrender of the southern part of Sakhalin to Russian jurisdiction.[31]

The Russian government, however, endeavored to pursue its traditional policy toward Korea, namely a 'waiting policy' even after the conclusion of the Kanghwa Treaty between Korea and

---

29) Byutsov to Gorchakov, Aug. 10 (22), 1873, Pak & Yureva (1973), pp. 172-173; Pak (1979), pp. 47-48.

30) Kopiya sekretnogo otnosheniya upravlyashchego ministerstvom inostamnykh del E. K. Byutsovu ot 26 sentyabrya (8 oktyabrya) 1873g. (Copy of Secret Letter sent to Byutsov by the Ministry of Foreign Affairs on Sept. 26 (Oct. 8), 1873), Pak & Yureva (1973), p. 173; Pak (1979), p. 48.

31) Narochnitskii (1956), pp. 257-258; Lensen (1982), 1, p. 12.

Japan. Such a Russian posture was clearly described in a memorandum of the Russian Foreign Ministry on the Korean question dated May 13, 1876. It runs as follows.

> Until this time, it did not occur [to us] to change the waiting policy, the guiding principle of the Ministry toward Korea, because all attempts by foreign powers to penetrate into this state remained unsuccessful. Even the present Japanese treaty [with Korea], in the opinion of the Ministry, does not call forth any necessity to take certain new measures, and our Ministry deems it better to maintain our former waiting policy given the present conditions. If other foreign states should want to follow the Japanese measures to renew their attempts to penetrate into Korea, Russia, as a neighbor with this state, could not remain an apathetic observer in the upheaval occurring in this state. If a certain foreign state concludes a treaty with Korea, then Russia would demand such a treaty [with Korea] in order to protect our interests in frontier trade and in future commerce.[32]

In the years 1875~76, when Korea confronted Japan, Russia was not in a position to pay any attention toward the Korean peninsula. Russia was caught in the heights of the Oriental crisis. In July 1875, revolutions broke out in Bosnia-Herzegovina, and the whole of the Balkan region was drawn into the vortex of war. The Russo-Turkish War of 1877 was approaching.

---

32) Zapiska ministerstva inostramnykh del o Koree ot 1 (13) maya 1876g. (Memorandum of the Ministry of Foreign Affairs relating to Korea dated May 1 (13), 1876), Pak & Yureva (1973), pp. 174-175; Pak (1979), p. 49.

The United States

During these turbulent years, America was not a world power like Great Britain or Russia. Nor was her interest in the Korean peninsula considerable, as that of China or Japan. Nonetheless, America made a serious intervention in Korean affairs which reslted in the conclusion of the first Korean treaty with the Western powers in 1882. The background of her active policy toward Korea lies in the American tradition whereby the Navy Department would play a leading role in expansionist foreign policy at that time.

J. A. Bingham, the U.S. Minister to Japan, did not pay any serious attention to the Korean-Japanese negotiations before the *Unyo* Incident of 1875. In this respect, his attitude was very different from that of H. Parkes, the British Minister to Japan.

After the *Unyo* Incident, Bingham reported to Washington, for the first time, concerning the Korean question. In this report, written on October 6, 1875, he wrote that he had learned from various sources that war may be declared by Japan against Korea. He also advised his government that, in the event of war, it would be proper for America to declare strict neutrality, although no treaty was in existence with Korea.[33] Bingham's negative attitude

---

33) Bingham to Fish, Oct. 6, 1875, FRUS, Japan, 1875, p. 348; AADM, pp. 875-876. The Department of the State preferred to issue a proclamation of neutrality only after active hostilities might be initiated. Treat (1938), I, p. 592.

was in exquisite contrast to Parkes' policy. Parkes pursued all possible benefits that were worth taking in the event of a conflict between Korea and Japan.

Immediately after deciding on Kuroda's dispatch to Korea, Terashima, the Japanese Minister of Foreign Affairs, made contact with the foreign diplomats residing in Tokyo and asked them for their cooperation. From the meeting with Terashima, Bingham inferred that if a treaty were not to be peacefully concluded, war would break out. He donated a book, the *Narrative* of *Perry's Expedition* to Terashima, judging that peaceful relations between Korea and Japan were desirable for America, and that Korea should be made amenable to reason.[34]

Bingham's negative attitude toward Korea became more stark, as illustrated in his reports to Washington after the conclusion of the Treaty of Commerce and Amity between Korea and Japan. He gathered information on Korea from Kuroda, and reported several times to his government, but his analysis of Korean-Japanese relations was not worth noting.[35]

Therefore, for information on Korea, the American government relied on reports from her embassy in Peking. F. Low, the American Minister to China, supplied the various sources with information regarding the Department of State, including Japanese newspapers, on the Korean-Japanese negotiations.[36] The

---

34) HISC, 1, pp. 42-55; Treat (1938), 1, pp. 592-593.
35) Bingham to Fish, Mar. 9, & Mar. 21, 1876, FRUS, 1876, Japan, pp. 370-371; AADM, pp. 876-877.
36) Low to Fish, Aug. 24, 1872 & Jan. 8, 1873, ADPP, 10, pp. 9-27.

retirement of the Taewŏnkun from the political scene and the process of the *Unyo* Incident were known to Washington only from the reports of S. W. William, acting Minister to China, and of B. P. Avery, the American Minister in Peking.[37]

But it was G. F. Seward who was able to supply better information on Korea to the State Department. He finally became Minister to China in January 1876, after finishing his long career as Consul-General in Shanghai. Just before proceeding to his new post, he sent J. L. Cadwalader, the Vice-Minister of State, a short but very comprehensive dispatch. In this report, Seward analysed the Korean situation as follows: if Japan did not occupy Korea permanently, China would not intervene in the Korean problems, and, as China treated Korea as an autonomous country, the conclusion of a treaty with Japan would fall under Korean discretionary power.[38] He also asked Bingham in Tokyo for an exchange of frank and candid opinions regarding Korea,[39] but the latter did not follow his advice.

In March 1876, immediately after the conclusion of the Korean-Japanese treaty, Seward again urged the State Department to empower him to reopen negotiations with Korea. But Fish replied: "it is not thought advisable at this moment to take any step in the direction of attempting negotiations with Korea. The subject and

---

37) Williams to Fish, Mar. 30, 1874, FRUS, 1874, China, pp. 253-254; ADPP, 10, pp. 28 ff.; AADM, pp. 874-875. Avery to Fish, Oct. 26, 1875, ADPP, 10, pp. 42-49.

38) Seward to Cadwalader, Dec. 28, 1875, ADPP, 10, pp. 50-52.

39) Seward to Bingham, Jan. 5, 1876, ADPP, 10, pp. 53-55.

your suggestions will be borne in mind."[40] Seward was very disappointed. Fish had an aversion toward Korea because of the experience of the American invasion of Korea in 1871. Therefore, negotiations with Korea would have to wait for a new minister in the State Department. In March 1877, Fish finally left the Department and the Korean question entered a new phase.

France and Germany

During those days when Korea and Japan confronted each other in 1875~76, France and Germany were not in a position to pay serious attention to the Korean peninsula. The French attitude toward Korea after the failure of her invasion in 1866 has been discussed by this author elsewhere in more detail.[41] After the defeat of France in the Franco-German War of 1870, the Far East was not the primary area of French political concern. She only sought the free propagation of Catholic doctrines in Korea through the successful achievement of the Japanese proposal to punish Korea (征韓論).

Upon hearing the news of the conclusion of the Korean-Japanese treaty, St. Quentin, the French chargé d'affaires in Tokyo, revealed a very negative and patronizing attitude. The treaty would be welcome "if only, unhappily, it was not to be feared that

---

40) Jones (1936), pp. 176-177.
41) Yongkoo Kim (2001), ch. 1.

this success will increase still more the pride of Japan in such a way as to render relations with that country more difficult, if not precarious."[42] He was not interested in the possible international repercussions the treaty might provoke. It was only at the end of the 1870s that France began to show renewed interest in Korea, and after the Franco-Chinese conflict over Vietnam in 1883-85, France became deeply involved in Far-Eastern problems.

After its unification, it was the basic German policy to keep the political status quo in Europe. Bismarck even loathed the word 'colony.' The initial motive toward the conclusion of the Korean-German treaty in 1882 came from the personal ambition of M. von Brandt, the German Minister to China. The actual negotiations between Korea and Germany were conducted under the umbrella of Great Britain. Active German involvement in Far-Eastern affairs thus came very late, when she took 'Weltpolitik' in 1890.

---

42) St. Quentin to Decazes, Mar. 11, 1876, Sims (1998), p. 116.

Conclusion

We have seen how Japan's distinctive perception of Korea historically embedded in its own society, finally materialized itself as a series of actual diplomatic policies after the Meiji Reformation.

When they adopted diplomatic policies toward Korea, the new leaders of the Meiji government capitalized on Western international law as a theoretical device through which they attempted to impose their own geo-political interests upon Korea.

I have argued that Meiji Japan was fundamentally expansionist from the very beginning, and that the "Korean question" was inexorably linked with the domestic political situation of Japan.

Korean leaders of the Chosŏn Dynasty, however, failed to understand this critical connection, or the changing nature of Japanese society. Moreover, they did not fully pay attention to the diplomatic strategies of the Western powers, which attempted to employ and support Japanese policies toward Korea. This limited understanding of the shifting international situation essentially stemmed from Korea's obstinate historical worldview.

It is fortunate that after experiencing the eight years' crisis from 1868 to 1876, there emerged a new political force, defined by the pursuit of an active diplomacy aimed at responding and adjusting to the new international environment. Historians call this new Korean political movement Kaehwapa (開化派, the enlightenment movement). With the formation of Kaehwapa, Korea's tremendous efforts to overcome their chronic "border thinking" had just begun.

Abbreviations

—

AADM: *Anglo-American Diplomatic Materials Relating to Korea, 1866-1886*, Park Il-Keun (Pak Ilgŭn, 朴日根) ed., Seoul, 1982.

ADPP: *American Diplomatic and Public Papers; The United States and China*, Davids, Jules, ed. Series II, *The United States, China, and Imperial Rivalries, 1861-1893*, Vol. 9-11, 3 vols., Wilmington, 1979.

BDFA: *British Documents of Foreign Affairs*, Part I Series E Vol. 1; *Japan and North-East Asia, 1860-1878*; Vol. 2; *Korea, the Ryukyu Islands, and North-East Asia, 1875-1888*, University Publication of America, 1989.

CCKJ: *Chŭngchŏng Kyorinji* (增訂交隣志, Enlarged and Revised Edition of Records of the Kyorin Order), Kim Kŏnsŏ (金健瑞) ed., 6 books, 3 vols., Seoul, 1802.

CYS: *Chouban yiwu shimo* (籌辦夷務始末, The Management of Barbarian Affairs, from A to Z), Gugong bowuyuan (故宮博物院), eds. 260 juan (卷), 1929-1930. Facsimile in 7 vols., Guofeng Publisher (國風出版社), Taiwan, 1963.

FRUS: *Foreign Relations of the United States.*

HICS: *Hanil oekyo migan kŭkpi saryo ch'ongsŏ* (韓日外交未刊極秘史料叢書, Classified Materials relating to Korean-Japanese Relations), Kim Yongkoo ed., 50 vols., Seoul, 1995-1996.

ISMJ: *Ilsa muncha* (日使文字, Documents of Japanese Envoys), T'ongsŏ (統署, Supreme Council), 1876. 1-1879. 6.

ISN: *Ilsŏngnok* (日省錄, Record of Daily Reflection), Kojong Period (高宗朝), Seoul taehakgyo kyuchanggak (서울대학교 규장각, Archival Library of Chosŏn Dynasty, Seoul National University), vols., 65-84, 1995-96.

ITKY: *Iltong kiyu* (日東記游, Record of a Journey to Japan), Kim Kisu (金綺秀), Seoul, 1971.

KHOM: *Kuhankuk oekyomunsŏ* (舊韓國外交文書, Diplomatic Documents of Old Korea), 24 vols., Seoul, 1966-1970.

KJSDS: *Kojong sidaesa* (高宗時代史, History of the Kojong Period), 5 vols., Kuksa p'yŏnch'an wiwŏnhoe (국사편찬위원회), Seoul, 1970.

KJSL: *Kojong sillok* (高宗實錄, Veritable Record of Kojong), 3 vols., Tamgudang (探究堂), Seoul, 1970.

KWCJ: *Kang Wi chŏn chip* (姜瑋全集, The Complete Works of Kang Wi), 2 vols., Seoul, 1978.

LGCC: *Li Wenchung gong chuanchi* (李文忠公全集, The Complete Works of Li Hungchang), 150 Books, Nanking, 1905. Reprinted in Taiwan, 7 vols., 1962.

NGB: *Nihon gaiko bunsho* (日本外交文書, Japanese Diplomatic Documents), Meiji Period, 73 vols., Japanese Ministry of Foreign Affairs, Tokyo, 1933-1963.

NGSS: *Nikan gaiko shiryo shusei* (日韓外交資料集成. A Compilation of Japan-Korean Diplomatic Materials), 10 vols., ed. by Kim Chŏngmyŏng (金正明), 1966.

PKSCJ: *Pak Kyusu Chŏnjip* (朴珪壽全集, The Complete Works of Pak Kyusu), 2 vols., Seoul, 1978.

QZRHGS: *Qingji Zhong Ri Han guanxi shiliao* (清季中日韓關係史料, Materials on Sino-Japanese-Korean Relations during the Late Qing Period), Jindaishi yanjiusuo (近代史研究所), 11 vols., Taiwan, 1972.

SJWIG: *Sŭngjŏngwŏn ilgi* (承政院日記, Records of the Royal Secretariat), Kojong Period (高宗朝), 15 vols., Kuksa p'yŏnch'an wiwŏnhoe (국사편찬위원회, National Historical Compilation Committee), Seoul, 1967-1968.

TMHG: *Tongmun hwigo* (同文彙考, Documents of the Common Ideographic Society), Kuksa p'yŏnch'an wiwŏnhoe (국사편찬위원회, National Historical Compilation Committee), Series on Korean Historical Materials (한국사료총서), no. 24, 4 vols., Seoul, 1978.

TMKJ: *T'ongmun Kwanji* (通文館志, Records of the Bureau of Interpreters), Kim Chinam (金指南) ed., 12 books, 6 vols., Seoul, 1888.

WSIG: *Waesa ilgi* (倭使日記, Diaries of Japanese Envoys), Ŭichŏngpu (議政府, the State Council), 14 vols., 1875. 12-1880. 12.

YHHN: *Yongho hannok* (龍湖閒錄, Casual Compilation of Yongho), Kuksa p'yŏnch'an wiwŏnhoe (국사편찬위원회, National Historical Compilation Committee), Series on Korean

Historical Materials (한국사료총서), no. 25, 1-3 vols., 1979, 4 vol., Seoul, 1980.

ZRJS: *Zhong-Ri jiaoshe shiliao, Qing Guangxuchao* (中日交涉史料. 清光緒朝, Materials on Sino-Japanese Negotiations during the Guangxu Reign), Gugong bowuyuan (故宮博物院) eds., 44 vols., 1932; 2 vols., Taiwan 1963.

ZRSM: *Zenrin shimatsu* (善隣始末, Good Neighborhood, from A to Z), 11 vols., Tokyo.

c; chinese

j; Japanese

k; Korean

Bibliography

Primary Sources

1. Korea

Sŭngjŏngwŏn ilgi (承政院日記, Records of the Royal Secretariat), Kojong Period (高宗朝), 15 vols., Kuksa p'yŏnch'an wiwŏnhoe (국사편찬위원회, National Historical Compilation Committee), Seoul, 1967-1968.

Ilsŏngnok (日省錄, Record of Daily Reflection), Kojong Period (高宗朝), (1) Seoul taehakgyo kochŏn kanhaenghoe (서울대학교 古典刊行會, Publishing Society of Classics, Seoul National University Library, Seoul, 1967-1972, 1982-1992, (2) Seoul taehakgyo kyuchanggak (서울대학교 규장각, Archival Library of Chosŏn Dynasty, Seoul National University), vols., 65-84, 1995-96.

Kojong sillok (高宗實錄, Veritable Record of Kojong), 3 vols., Tamgudang (探究堂), Seoul, 1970.

Pibyŏnsa tŭngnok (備邊司謄錄, Record of the Border Defence Command), Kojong Period (高宗朝), vols, 36-7, Kuksa p'yŏnch'an wiwŏnhoe (국사편찬위원회), Seoul, 1960.

Tongmun hwigo (同文彙考, Documents of the Common Ideographic Society), Kuksa p'yŏnch'an wiwŏnhoe (국사편찬위원회), Series on

Korean Historical Materials (한국사료총서), no. 24, 4 vols., Seoul, 1978.

T'ongmun Kwanji (通文館志, Records of the Bureau of Interpreters), Kim Chinam (金指南) ed., 12 books, 6 vols, Seoul, 1888.

Chŭngchŏng Kyorinji (增訂交隣志, Enlarged and Revised Edition of Records of the Kyorin Order), Kim Kŏnsŏ (金健瑞) ed., 6 books, 3 vols., Seoul, 1802.

Waesa ilgi (倭使日記, Diaries of Japanese Envoys), Ŭichŏngpu (議政府, the State Council), 14 vols., 1875. 12-1880. 12.

Ilsa muncha (日使文字, Documents of Japanese Envoys), T'ongsŏ (統署, Supreme Council), 1876.1-1879. 6.

Kuhankuk oekyomunsŏ (舊韓國外交文書, Diplomatic Documents of Old Korea), 24 vols., Seoul, 1966-1970.

Yongho hannok (龍湖閒錄, Casual Compilation of Yongho), Kuksa p'yŏnch'an wiwŏnhoe (국사편찬위원회), Series on Korean Historical Materials (한국사료총서), no. 25, 1-3 vols., 1979, 4 vol., Seoul, 1980.

Kojong sidaesa (高宗時代史, History of the Kojong Period), 5 vols., Kuksa p'yŏnch'an wiwŏnhoe (국사편찬위원회), Seoul, 1970.

Kang Wi (姜瑋), *Kang Wi chŏn chip* (姜瑋全集, The Complete Works of Kang Wi), 2 vols., Seoul, 1978.

Kim Kisu (金綺秀), *Iltong kiyu* (日東記游, Record of a Journey to Japan), Seoul, 1971.

Kim yunsik (金允植), *Kim yunsik chŏnjip* (金允植全集, The Complete Works of Kim Yunsik), 2 vols., Seoul, 1980.

Pak Kyusu (朴珪壽), *Pak Kyusu Chŏnjip* (朴珪壽全集, The Complete Works of Pak Kyusu), 2 vols., Seoul, 1978.

2. China

Chouban yiwu shimo (籌辦夷務始末, The Management of Barbarian Affairs,

from A to Z), Gugong bowuyuan (故宮博物院), eds. 260 juan (卷),
1929-1930. Facsimile in 7 vols., Guofeng Publisher (國風出版社),
Taiwan, 1963. A punctuated edition of Daoguangchao (道光朝) and
of Xianfengchao (咸豐朝) was put out by Zhonghua (中華) Publisher
in 1964 and 1979 respectively. Beijing daxue (北京大學), reprint, 9
vols., 1981.

Qingji Zhong Ri Han guanxi shiliao (清季中日韓關係史料, Materials on
Sino-Japanese-Korean Relations during the Late Qing Period),
Jindaishi yanjiusuo (近代史研究所), 11 vols., Taiwan, 1972.

Zhong Ri jiaoshe shiliao, Qing Guangxuchao (中日交涉史料. 清光緒朝,
Materials on Sino-Japanese Negotiations during the Guangxu
Reign), Gugong bowuyuan (故宮博物院) eds., 44 vols., 1932; 2 vols.,
Taiwan 1963.

Li Wenchung gong chuanchi (李文忠公全集, The Complete Works of Li
Hungchang), 150 Books, Nanking, 1905. Reprinted in Taiwan, 7
vols., 1962. 9 vols., 1980. Li Hungchang chuanchi (李鴻章全集),
Shanghai, 5 vols., 1985-, Subsequent volumes would facilitate the
use of as yet unpublished sources in the Shanghai Library.

3. Japan

Nihon gaiko bunsho (日本外交文書, Japanese Diplomatic Documents),
Meiji Period, 73 vols., Japanese Ministry of Foreign Affairs, Tokyo,
1933-1963.

Hanil oekyo migan kŭkpi saryo ch'ongsŏ (韓日外交未刊極秘史料叢書,
Classified Materials relating to Korean-Japanese Relations), Kim
Yongkoo (김용구) ed., 50 vols., Seoul, 1995-6.

Nikan gaiko shiryo shusei (日韓外交資料集成. A Compilation of Japan-
Korean Diplomatic Materials), 10 vols., ed. by Kim Chŏngmyŏng
(金正明), 1966.

Zenrin shimatsu (善隣始末, Good Neighborhood, from A to Z), 11 vols., Tokyo.

Chosen Jimusho (朝鮮事務書, Books on Korean Affairs), Nihon Gaimusho (日本外務省), 1867-1874, Facsimile in 9 vols., Pusan, 1971.

4. Great Britain

British Documents of Foreign Affairs, Part I Series E Vol. 1; *Japan and North-East Asia, 1860-1878*; Vol. 2; *Korea, the Ryukyu Islands, and North-East Asia, 1875-1888*, University Publication of America, 1989.

Anglo-American Diplomatic Materials Relating to Korea, 1866-1886, Park Il-Keun (Pak Ilgŭn, 朴日根) ed., Seoul, 1982.

5. The United States

Foreign Relations of the United States.

American Diplomatic and Public Papers; The United States and China, Davids, Jules, ed. Series II, *The United States, China, and Imperial Rivalries, 1861-1893*, Vol. 9-11, 3 vols., Wilmington, 1979.

Secondary Sources

Arano Yasunori (荒野泰典), *Kinsei nihon to higasi asia* (近世日本と東アジア, Modern Japan and East Asia), Tokyo, 1988.

Coates, P. D., *China Consuls*, Oxford, 1988.

Daniels, Gordon, *Sir Harry Parkes, British Representative in Japan, 1865-83*, Japan Library, 1996.

Elisonas, Jurgis, "The Inseparable Trinity: Japan's Relations with China and Korea," *The Cambridge History of Japan*, 4, 1991, pp. 235-372.

Harada Tamaki (原田環), *Chosen no gaikok to kindaika* (朝鮮の開國と近代
化, The Opening of Korea and Modernization), Hiroshima, 1997.

Jones, Frances C., *Foreign Diplomacy in Korea, 1866-1894*, Harvard Univ.
Ph. D. dissertation, 1936.

Kim Yongkoo (金容九), Ch'um ch'unǔn hoeǔi. Pinhoeǔi oekyo (춤추는 회
의. 빈 회의 외교. The Congress Dances. Diplomacy at the Congress
of Vienna), Seoul, 1997.

_____, *Segyegwan ch'ugdol ǔi kukchejǒngch'ihak* (세계관 충돌의 국제정치
학, The Clash of Worldviews and International Politics), Seoul,
1997.

_____, *Sekyekwan ch'ungdol kwa hanmal oekyosa, 1866-1882* (세계관 충
돌과 한말 외교사, 1866-1882, The Clash of Worldviews and
Diplomatic History in the late Chosǒn Dynasty), 서울, 2001.

_____, *Segye oegyosa* (세계외교사, World Diplomatic History), 9th rev. ed.,
Seoul, 2005.

_____, et al., eds, Hankuk oekyosa yǒnku. Munhǒn haechae (한국 외교사
연구. 문헌해제. A Study of Korean Diplomatic History. An annotated
Bibliography), Seoul, 1996.

Lensen, George A., *Korea and Manchuria between Japan and Russia*,
Tallahasse, 1966.

_____, *Balance of Intrigue. International Rivalry in Korea &
Manchuria, 1884-1899,* 2 vols., Tallahasse, 1982.

Min Dǒkki (閔德基), Higashiajia no nakano kannichi kankei (東アジアのなか
の韓日關係, Korean-Japanese Relations in the East Asia), Tokyo,
1994.

Nakamura Hidetaka (中村榮孝), Nissen kankeishi no kenkyu (日鮮關係史の
研究, A Study of Japan-Korean Relations), 3 vols., Tokyo, 1965-
1969.

Narochnitskii, A. L.. *Kolonialnaya politika kapitalisticheskikh derzhav na dalnem vostoke, 1860-1895* (The Colonial Politics of the Capitalist Powers in the Far East, 1860-1895), Moskva, 1956.

Pak, Boris D. & G. N. Yureva, "Rossiya i borba derzhav za otkrytie Korei v 1866-1876 gg." (Russia and Struggle of Powers for the Opening of Korea, 1866-1876), *Ocherki Istorii Sibiri*. Vypusk 3, 1973 (Ministrestvo prosveshcheniya RSFSR. Irkuskii gosudarstvennyi pedagogicheskii institut, Irkusk)(Outlines of Siberian History, no. 3. Ministry of Education, Russian Socialist Federation of Soviet Republics, National Institut of Pedagogy, Irkustk)

Pak, Boris D., "Russko-Koreiiskii dogovor 1884" (Russo-Korean Treaty, 1884), *Ocherki istorii Sibiri*, Vyp. 2, 1971 (Outlines of Siberian History), Ministerstvo proveshcheniya RSFSR. Irkuskii gosudarstven-nyi pedagogicheskii institut, (Ministry of Education, Russian Socialist Federation of Soviet Republics, National Institut of Pedagogy, Irkustk), Irkusk, pp. 136-161.

_____, "Kim Okkyun i Rossiya" (Kim Okkyun and Russia), *Narodny Azii i Afriki* (Peoples of Asia and Africa), no. 3, 1974, pp. 135-140.

_____, *Rossiya i Koreya* (Russia and Korea), Moskva, 1979.

Peng (彭澤周), Meijishoki niseikan kankei no kenkyu (明治初期日清韓關係の研究, A Study of Japan-China-Korean Relations in the Early Meiji Period), Tokyo, 1969.

Sim Kichae (沈箕載), *Bakmatsu nichogaikoshi no kenkyu* (幕末維新日朝外交史の研究, A Study of Japanese-Korean Diplomatic History in the late Bakfu and Early Reforma-tion), Kyoto, 1997.

Sims, Richard, *French Policy towards the Bakufu and Meiji Japan, 1854-95*, Japan Library, 1998.

Tabohashi Kyoshi (田保橋潔), *Kindai nissen kankei no genkyu* (近代日鮮關係の研究, A Study on Modern Japanese-Korean Relations), 2 vols., Seoul, 1940.

Tokutomi Iitsiro (德富猪一郎), Koshaku Yamagata Aritomo ten (公爵山縣有

朋傳, A Biography of Duke Yamagata Aritomo), 3 vols., Tokyo, 1933.

Treat, Payson J., *Diplomatic Relations between the United States and Japan*, 3 vols., Stanford, 1938.

Yamabe Kentaro (山邊健太郎), Nihon no kankok heiggo (日本の韓國併合, Japanese Annexation of Korea), Tokyo, 1970.

Yi Hun (李熏), "Chosŏn hugi taeil oegyomunsŏ" (朝鮮後期 對日外交文書, Diplomatic Documents to Japan in the Latter Period of Chosŏn Dynasty), *Komunsŏ yŏnku* (『古文書研究』, Studies on Old Documents), no. 4, 1993, pp. 51-78.

Yi Kwangrin (李光麟), *Hankuk kehwasa yŏnku* (韓國開化史研究, A Study of Korean Enlightenment History), Seoul, 1969.

_____, *Kehwatang yŏnku* (開化黨研究, A Study of Enlightenment Party), Seoul, 1973.

_____, *Hankuk kehwasasang yŏnku* (韓國開化思想研究, A Study of Korean Enlightenment Thought), Seoul, 1979.

_____, *Kehwaki ŭi inmul* (開化期의 人物, Great Men in the Enlighten-ment Period), Seoul, 1993.

_____, *Kehwaki yŏnku* (開化期研究, A Study of Enlightenment Period), Seoul, 1994.

Index-Glossary

(A)

Abolition of Domains, see
　　Haihanchiken (j. 廢藩置縣)
additional articles, see purok (k. 附
　　録)
Amur　130
An Tongjun (安東晙)　21, 25-27,
　　39, 43, 44
annual trading ship, see
　　sekyŏnsŏn (k. 歲遣船)
Arakawa Tokushi (荒川德滋)　110
arguments over whether to con-
　　quer Korea, see seikanron (j.
　　征韓論)
Ariadne, the　130
army commander, see ch'ŏmsa(k.
　　僉使)
Ashikaga Yoshimitsu (足利義滿)

5

assistant language official, see
　　pyŏlch'ahundo (k. 別差訓導)
autonomy, see chachu (k. 自主)
Avery, Benjamin P.　142

(B)

Baodingpu (保定府)　68, 69
Bakufu (j. 幕府)　3, 4, 10
Beiyang dachen (c. 北洋大臣,
　　Superintendent for the
　　Northern Ports)　68, 126
Belcher, Edward　133
Berlin　132
Bingham, John Amos　140-142
Bismarck, Otto von　144
Board of Punishments, Chosŏn,
　　see Hyŏngcho (k. 刑曹)
Board of Rites, Chinese, see Lifu

(c. 禮部)

Board of Rites, Chosŏn, see Yecho (k. 禮曹)

Boissonade, Gustave Emile   66

border thinking   148

Bosnia-Herzegovina   139

Brandt, Max von   144

Byutsov, Evgenii K.   137, 138

(C)

Cabinet Councilor, see sangi (j. 參議)

Cadwalader, John L.   142

chachu (k. 自主, autonomy)   69, 82, 83

ch'apiyŏkkwan (k. 差備譯官, temporary translator)   114

ch'amp'an (k. 參判, second minister)   10, 27

ch'amŭi (k. 參議, third minister)   10, 103

Chefoo (芝罘)   75, 131

chichon (k. 至尊, the Most Revered)   42

Chief Magistrate of Seoul Magistracy, see Hansŏngpuyun (k. 漢城府尹)

Chief Minister of the Office of Royal Relatives, see

Yŏngtonyŏngpusa (k. 領敦寧府事)

Chief Minister of the Office of Senior Officials without Portfolio, see p'anchungch'upusa (k. 判中樞府事)

Chief State Councilor, see Yŏngŭichŏng (k. 領議政)

ch'ik (k. 勅, edict)   20, 24, 28, 29, 41

Cho Inhŭi (趙寅熙)   90, 114-116, 118, 119

Ch'oi Ikhyŏn (崔益鉉)   102

Ch'ojijin (k. 草芝鎭, Ch'oji fortress)   61, 62

ch'ŏmsa (k. 僉使, army commander)   33

chŏnkwŏn (k. 全權, full powers)   73, 74, 77, 97, 99, 113, 114

Chŏng Hyŏndŏk (鄭顯德)   20, 21, 33, 39, 44

Ch'ŏncha (k. 天子, the Son of Heaven)   41, 46, 49

Chong Hou (崇厚)   67

chŏngkyogumryŏng (k. 政教禁令, government exhortations and restrictions)   67, 124

Chŏnra (全羅)   87, 88

chŏpkyŏn taesin (k. 接見大臣,

Minister of Reception) 72

Ch'oryang (草梁) 12, 25, 86

chosin(k. 朝臣, imperial subject)
20, 26, 27, 29

Chu (楚) 52, 113

chukwŏn (k. 主權, sovereignty)
83, 89

Ch'ungch'ŏng (忠淸) 87, 88

Chungch'upu(k. 中樞府, the Office
of Senior Officials without
Portfolio) 98, 125

chwaŭichŏng (k. 左議政, the second state councilor) 48

Commanding General of Ŏyŏng
Regiment, see Ŏyŏng
Taechang (k. 御營大將)

communication envoy, see
Tongsinsa (k. 通信使)

Consular Jurisdiction (領事裁判)
91

Council of State, see Dajokan (j. 太
政官)

(D)

Daimyo (大名) 6

Dajodaijin (j. 太政大臣, Prime
Minister) 38, 65

Dajokan (j. 太政官, the Council of
State) 30, 31

Date Munenari (伊達宗城) 23

dealing with the neighbor, see
Kyorin (k. 交隣)

Deputy Commander, see
p'uch'ongkwan (k. 副摠官)

Derby, Edward Stanley 128, 133,
135-137

diplomatic document under the
Kyorin order, see sŏgye (k. 書
契)

Disturbance of the Three Ports,
see Samporan (k. 三浦亂)

Dong Xun (董恂) 67, 68

(E)

edict, see ch'ik (k. 勅)

Edo (江戶) 3, 6-10

emperor, see hwang (k. 皇)

enriching the nation and strengthening the army, see
pugukkangpyŏng (k. 富國強
兵)

Exploration Commissioner, see
Kaitakudaijin (j. 開拓長官)

(F)

fan (j. 藩, domain) 9, 20, 22, 24,
26, 27, 29, 30, 32, 33

Fish, Hamilton   140-143

Franco-German War of 1870   143

full powers, see chŏnkwŏn (k. 全權)

(G)

Gaikokukan (j. 外國官, the Japanese Ministry of Foreign Affairs, 1868-1869)   22, 23

Genbo (玄方)   8

General Sherman Incident, the (1866)   40, 108

Genroin Gikan (j. 元老院 議官, Senate Councilor)   71

Gorchakov, Aleksandr M.   137, 138

government exhortations and restrictions, see chŏngkyo-gumryŏng (政教禁令)

Governor of Pyŏngan Province, see Pyŏngando Kwanch'alsa (k. 平安道觀察使)

Governor of Zhili Province, see Zhili Zongdu (c. 直隷總督)

grandee of Kyushu   4

Guangzhou (廣州)   12

guard, see pantang (k. 伴倘)

Guo Songtao (郭嵩燾)   67, 68

(H)

Hachinohe Junshuku (八戶順叔)   67, 68, 74

Haihanchiken (j. 廢藩置縣, Abolition of Domains)   32, 37, 38, 64

Haikuo tuchi (c. 海國圖志, *Illustrated Treatise on the Sea Kingdoms*)   107

Hakodate, the (函館)   71

Hamgyŏng (咸慶)   87, 88

Hanabusa Yoshimoto (花房義質)   34, 117

Hansŏngpuyun (k. 漢城府尹, Chief Magistrate of Seoul Magistracy)   40

Hei Long River (黑龍江)   111

Higuchi Tetsushiro (樋口鐵四郎)   25

Hira Yoshiaki (平義達)   20

Hirotsu Hironobu (廣津弘信)   32, 33, 59, 60

hoedapgyŏmswaehwansa (k. 回答兼刷還使, response and repatriation embassy)   9

hoedapsa (k. 回答使, response embassy)   9

Hong Sunmok (洪淳穆)   52

Hukami Masakage (深見正景) 34

hundo (k. 訓導, language official)
20, 21, 25, 43, 44, 46, 61, 72,
96

husŏ (k. 後敍, postscript) 105

Hyŏn Sŏkun (玄昔運) 44, 50, 61,
72, 96, 99, 101, 103

Hyŏngcho (k. 刑曹, Chosŏn Board
of Punishments) 40, 114

hwang (k. 皇, emperor) 20, 23,
24, 28, 29, 41, 43, 45, 46, 49,
52, 82

Hwang Chŏngyŏn (黃正淵) 49,
50

(I)

Iltongkiyu (k. 『日東記游』, *Record
of a Journey to Japan*) 105,
107, 109

Imjin War (k. 壬辰倭亂, 1592-1598)
4, 7, 8, 9

Imo kunran (k. 壬午軍亂, Imo
Military Uprising of 1882)
117

imperial subject, see chosin (朝臣)

Imsin Agreement (k. 壬申約條,
1512) 6-8

Incheon (仁川) 61, 62, 72-74, 88,
99

independence, see tokrip (k. 獨立)

Inoue Kaoru (井上馨) 71, 78,
103, 108, 111

Inoue Kowashi (井上毅) 66

Inoue Yoshika (井上良馨) 62, 63

Ito Hirobumi (伊藤博文) 66

(J)

Japanese brigands, see waeku (k.
倭寇)

Japan House, see waekwan (k. 倭
館)

Jiyutoshi (『自由黨史』) 62

(K)

kaehangka (k. 開港家, promoter of
the opening of ports) 97

kaehwapa (k. 開化派, progressive
party) 50, 97, 99, 148

Kaitakudaijin (j. 開拓長官,
Exploration Commissioner)
71

kamhapmuyŏk (k. 勘合貿易, tally
trade) 5, 11

Kang Wi (姜瑋) 50, 99

Kanghwado (k. 江華島, Kanghwa
Island) 61, 62, 70-72, 78, 88,
92, 97, 99, 101, 111, 124

Kanghwadosakŏn (k. 江華島事件, Kanghwa Incident) 56, 60-67, 70, 73, 74, 127, 140, 142

Kanghwado Treaty (k. 江華島條約, the Treaty of Amity and Commerce between Korea and Japan, 1876) 19, 59, 95, 103, 114, 116, 123, 136-138, 141, 142

kangsukwan (k. 講修官, treaty negotiator) 114

Kawamoto Kusaemon (川本九左衛門) 22, 24, 25

Kawamura Smiyoshi (川村純義) 63

Kido Takayoshi (木戶孝允) 32, 65

Kim Ch'ŏlgyun (金徹均) 33

Kim Hongjip (金弘集) 117

Kim Kisu (金綺秀) 95, 102-114

Kim Kyeun (金繼運) 54

Kim Pyŏngguk (金炳國) 48, 49, 51, 53, 54, 98

Kim Pyŏnghak (金炳學) 98

Kim Saeho (金世鎬) 21

Kiyu Agreement (k. 己酉約條, 1609) 7, 8

Kojong, King (k. 高宗) 19, 38-42, 44-51, 54, 74, 77, 95, 96, 98, 102, 104, 105, 108, 113, 117, 125, 126

Kŏmundo (k. 巨文島, Port Hamilton) 123, 127-137

Kyoru, the (矯龍) 71

Komatsu Tatewaki (小松帶刀) 22, 23

Kung, Prince (恭親王) 67

Kuroda Kyotaka (黑田清隆) 71, 73-78, 85, 88, 89, 91, 103, 108, 141

Kwangbok Tong (光復洞) 12

Kyehae Agreement (癸亥約條, 1443) 5-7

Kyŏnggi (京畿) 87, 88

Kyŏngnam (慶南) 87

Kyŏngsang (慶尙) 21, 88

Kyorin (k. 交隣, dealing with the neighbor) 3-5, 7, 8, 10, 13, 17, 18, 27-30, 34, 43, 45, 47, 52-55, 59, 73, 74, 81, 83-85, 90, 95, 100, 102-105, 115, 117, 123

Kyoto (京都) 22

Kyushu (九州) 3-6

(L)

Landeshoheit 83

language official, see hundo (k. 訓導)

li (c. 禮, proper ceremonial forms)
77

Lifu (c. 禮部, Chinese Board of
Rites)   74, 83, 124, 126

Li Hungchang (李鴻章)   68-70,
124-126

Liqing (c. 禮經, The Classic of li)
73

Low, Frederick   141

Lu (魯)   113

(M)

Margary Incident   69

Mayers, W. S. F.   128

Meiji Restoration (明治維新)   3, 4,
7, 10-13, 18, 22, 64, 104, 147

Military Headquarters, see
Toch'ongpu (k. 都總府)

Miyamoto Koichi (宮本小一)   72,
78, 86, 90, 96, 97, 107, 114,
115, 118, 119

Ming (明)   5, 8, 11, 124

Minister, see p'anso (k. 判書)

Minister of Reception, see
chŏpkyŏn taesin (k. 接見大臣)

Mohwa Kwan (k. 慕華館,
Commemoration House for
the Chinese)   126

Mori Arinori (森有禮)   66-70

Moriyama Shigeru (森山茂)   32-
34, 38, 39, 43, 45, 48, 54, 56,
59, 60, 70, 72, 95, 107, 108,
124, 133, 137

Most Revered, the, see chichon (k.
至尊)

most-favored-nation clause   92

Mosung, the (孟春)   71

Mt. Yongdu (龍頭山)   12

munkyŏnpyŏltan (k. 聞見別單, special report on facts heard and
seen)   105, 109

munin (k. 文引, trading permit)
6, 8

munuisa (k. 問慰使, special inquiring and consolatory official)
9

(N)

Nagasaki (長崎)   4, 24, 61, 63

Naeip'o (乃而浦, nowadays
Chinhae 鎭海)   7

Nakai Koso (中井弘藏)   22

Newchang (牛莊)   61-63

Nitsin, the (日進)   71, 72

(O)

O (吳)   52

O Kyŏngsŏk (吳慶錫)　50, 55, 72,
　96, 97, 101, 111
Office for the General Manage-
　ment of Affairs concerning the
　Various Countries, see Zongli
　Yamen (c. 總理衙門, 總理各國
　通商事務衙門)
Office of Interpreters, see
　Sayŏkwŏn (k. 司譯院)
Office of Royal Relatives, see
　Tonryŏngpu (k. 敦寧府)
Office of Senior Officials without
　Portfolio, see Chungch'upu (k.
　中樞府)
Official with the rank above
　upper-senior third-grade, see
　tangsangkwan (k. 堂上官)
Okugi Isamu (奧義制)　34, 38
Opium War (1839-1842)　12, 18
Osaka (大阪)　22
Oshima Tomonoso (大島友之允)
　22
Ouchi (大內)　6
Ŏyŏng Taechang (k. 御營大將,
　Commanding General of
　Ŏyŏng Regiment)　72

(P)

Pak Kyusu (朴珪壽)　38, 40-43,

　46, 50, 51, 55, 98, 99, 108
p'anchungch'upusa (k. 判中樞府事,
　Chief Minister of the Office of
　Senior Officials without
　Portfolio)　52, 98
p'ansŏ (k. 判書, Minister)　27, 40
pantang (k. 伴倘, guard)　99
Pang Usŏ (方禹叙)　41
Parkes, Harry　127-137, 140, 141
Peking (北京)　4, 67, 125, 128,
　141, 142
Perry, Mathew Calbraith　10, 135,
　141
Plunkett, F. R.　133
postscript, see husŏ (k. 後敍)
Prime Minister, see Dajodaijin (j.
　太政大臣)
Port Hamilton, see Kŏmundo (k.
　巨文島)
Prefect of Tongrae Prefecture, see
　Tongraepusa (k. 東萊府使)
Progressive Party, see kaehwapa
　(k. 開化派)
Public Law of All Nations, see
　wankuokongfa (c. 萬國公法)
p'uch'ongkwan (k. 副摠官, Deputy
　Commander)　72
pugukkangpyŏng (k. 富國强兵,
　enriching the nation and
　strengthening the army)　109

Pup'yŏng (富平) 73, 99

purok (附錄, additional articles)
87, 92, 114

Pusan (釜山) 4, 7-9, 12, 13, 31-
33, 44, 45, 61, 63, 71, 72, 86,
88, 90, 98, 103, 104, 117, 133,
135

pyŏlch'ahundo (k. 別差訓導, assistant language official) 20,
25, 71

Pyŏngan Province (平安道) 40

Pyŏngando Kwanch'alsa (k. 平安道
觀察使, Governor of Pyŏngan
Province) 40, 41

(Q)

Qi (薺) 113

Qin (秦) 113

Quentin, St. 143, 144

(R)

response and repatriation embassy,
see hoedapgyŏmswaehwansa
(k. 回答兼刷還使)

response embassy, se hoedapsa
(k. 回答使)

Russo-Turkish War of 1877 139

Ryder, Alfred P. 130-132

(S)

Sadae (k. 事大, serving the superi-
or) 3, 5, 18, 24, 37, 65, 68,
83

Sagara Masaki (相良正樹) 33, 34

Saigo Takamori (西鄉隆盛) 63

St. Petersburg 132

Sakhalin 129, 130, 135, 138

Samporan (k. 三浦亂, Disturbance
of the Three Ports, 1510) 6

samtae (k. 三擡), see *taetu*

sangtae (k. 雙擡), see *taetu*

Sanjo Sanetomi (三條實美) 38, 65

sangi (j. 參議, Cabinet Councilor)
65, 71

sangpyŏngchŏn (k. 常平錢, Korean
copper coins) 100

Sata Hakubo (佐田白茅) 31

Satow, Ernest 108

Satsuma clan (j. 薩摩藩) 62, 63

Sayŏkwŏn (k. 司譯院, Office of
Interpreters) 72

seal, see *tosŏ* (k. 圖書)

second minister, see ch'am'an (k.
參判)

second state councilor, see
chwaŭichŏng (k. 左議政)

seikanron (j. 征韓論, arguments

over whether to conquer
Korea)   34, 39, 64, 65, 143
sekyŏnsŏn (k. 歲遣船, annual trad-
ing ship)   6, 8
Senate Councilor, see Genroin
Gikan (j. 元老院 議官)
serving the superior, see *Sadae* (k.
事大)
Seward, George F.   142, 143
Shanghai   131, 142
Shen Guifen (沈桂芬)   67
Seoul   4, 8, 40, 41, 71, 85, 88, 99,
101, 114-117, 126
Shadwell, Charles F. A.   129, 131
Shogun (將軍)   5-8, 10
Silver Road   4
Sin Hŏn (申櫶)   72-74, 76-78, 86,
99-103, 108, 111, 112, 114-116
Sŏ Taemun (k. 西大門, West Gate)
116, 126
So Yoshiaki (宗義達)   12, 22, 23,
33
Soejima Taneomi (副島種臣)   137,
138
sŏgye (k. 書契, diplomatic document under the *Kyorin* order)
10-13, 17, 19-22, 24, 26-28, 34,
40-56, 61, 64, 73-75, 96, 101,
115
sŏk (k. 石, j; *koku*, one sŏk = 5.119

bushels)   6, 8
Son of Heaven, see Ch'ŏncha (k.
天子)
Song (宋)   113
sovereignty, see chukwŏn (k. 主
權)
special inquiring and consolatory
official, see munuisa (k. 問慰
使)
special report on facts heard and
seen, see munkyŏnpyŏltan (k.
聞見別單)
Spring and Autumn (春秋)   52,
113
State Council, see Ŭichŏngpu (k.
議政府)
Suchŏngchŏn (修政殿, the Hall of
Political Affairs)   97
sujikin (k. 受職人, office-holder
endowed by the Korean
court)   7
Superintendent for the Northern
Ports, see Beiyang dachen (北
洋大臣)
susachaetan (k. 隨事裁斷, discretion to decide according to
circumstances)   99
suzerainty · 65-70
Sylvia, the   131

(T)

Taepu Island (大阜島)　72

taetu (k. 擡頭, c; *taitou*. elevation of one letter to express deference to a superior)　11

Taewŏngun (大院君)　19, 21, 37-42, 46, 47, 55, 60, 96, 101, 102, 142

tally trade, see kamhapmuyŏk (k. 勘合貿易)

tangsangkwan (k. 堂上官, official with the rank above upper-senior third-grade)　50, 72, 98, 103

tantae (單擡), see taetu

Tei Einei (鄭永寧)　66

temporary translator, see ch'apiyŏkkwan (差備譯官)

Terashima Munenori (寺島宗則)　66, 127, 137, 141

third minister, see ch'amŭi (k. 參議)

Third State Councilor, see Uŭichŏng (k. 右議政)

Tientsin (天津),　68

Ting (唐)　41

Toch'ongpu (k. 都總府, Military Headquarters)　72

tokrip (k. 獨立, independence)　83

Tokugawa Iemasa (德川家定)　10

Tokugawa Ieyasu (德川家康)　7

Tokugawa Ieyoshi (德川家慶)　9

Tokyo (東京)　55, 75, 85, 127, 133, 141, 142

Tongraepu (k. 東萊府, Tongrae Prefecture)　20, 46, 49

Tongraepusa (k. 東萊府使, Prefect of Tongrae Prefecture)　20, 21, 33, 38, 47-49, 55, 56, 117

Tongsangchangchŏng (k. 通商章程, Trade Regulations)　92, 114, 118, 119

Tonryŏngpu (k. 敦寧府, Office of Royal Relatives)　98

Tongsinsa (k. 通信使, literally 'communication envoy')　8-10, 84, 85, 103, 104

tosŏ (k. 圖書, seal)　5, 8, 10-13, 42

Trade Regulations, see Tongsangchangchŏng (k. 通商章程)

Trading Factory (海外商館)　12

trading permit, see munin (k. 文引)

Treaty of Amity and Commerce between Korea and Japan, 1876, see Kanghwado Treaty (k. 江華島條約)

treaty negotiator, see kangsukwan (k. 講修官)

Tsushima (對馬島)　3-12, 19, 20, 22-34, 41, 43, 45, 53-56, 63, 133, 134

(U)

Ŭichŏngpu (k. 議政府, the State Council)　20, 49, 50, 54, 101

Ŭichu (義州)　4

Ŭng Island (鷹島)　62

Unyo, the (雲揚號), see Kanghwadosakŏn (k. 江華島事件, Kanghwa Incident)

Urase Hiroshi (浦瀬裕)　26, 29, 110

Uŭichŏng (k. 右議政, the Third State Councilor)　43, 48, 98

(V)

Vladivostok　130

(W)

Wade, Thomas F.　130

waeku (k. 倭寇, Japanese brigands)　5, 6

waekwan (k. 倭館, Japan House)　7, 12, 13, 25, 26, 31, 33, 34, 38, 43, 46-49, 71

waeyangilch'ae (k. 倭洋一體, Japan and the West are one)　47

waifan (c. 外藩, external vassal)　83, 123

wankuokongfa (c. 萬國公法, Public Law of All Nations)　69, 76, 77, 113

wankuoputongzhifa (c. 萬國普通之法, Common Law of All Nations)　77

Warring States (戰國)　113

Wei (衛)　113

western learning, see yanghak (k. 洋學)

William, S. Wells　142

Wŏlmi Island (月尾島)　62

Wŏnsan (元山)　88, 135

(Y)

Yamagata Aritomo (山縣有朋)　63

Yamanojo Skenaga (山之城祐長)　71

Yanagihara Sakimitsu (柳原前光)　32

yanghak (k. 洋學, western learning)　106

Yecho (禮曹, Chosŏn Board of

Rites) 10, 12, 21, 28, 44, 45, 74, 84, 85, 103

Yi Ch'oeŭng (李最應) 41, 48, 53, 55, 98

Yi Chuhyŏn (李周鉉) 25, 27

Yi Chunsu (李濬秀) 71

Yi Tongin (李東仁) 108

Yi Yongsuk (李容肅) 103, 109, 110, 114

Yi Yuwŏn (李裕元) 43, 45, 51, 54, 98, 125, 126

Yinghuan chiluel (c.『瀛環志略』, Record of the Ocean Circuit) 107

Yokohama (橫濱) 131

Yŏmp'o (鹽浦, nowadays Ulsan 蔚山) 7

Yŏnhŭng (永興) 88

Yŏngjong Island (永宗島) 61, 74

Yŏngŭichŏng (k. 領議政, the Chief State Councilor) 43, 51, 55, 98

Yŏngtonyŏngpusa (k. 領敦寧府事, Chief Minister of the Office of Royal Relatives) 98

Yŏnmutae (k. 練武臺, Military Training Camp) 73, 78

Yoshioka Koki (吉岡弘毅) 32, 33

Yun Chasŭng (尹滋丞) 72, 77, 114, 116, 124

(Z)

Zhang Sigui (張斯桂) 113

Zheng (鄭) 113

Zheng Jishi (鄭基世) 126

Zhili Zongdu (c. 直隷總督, Governor of Zhili Province) 68, 69

Zongli Yamen (c. 總理衙門, 總理各國通商事務衙門, The Office for the General Management of Affairs concerning the Various Countries) 67-70, 124-126

Korea and Japan
The Clash of Worldviews, 1868-1876

2006년 11월 30일 초판 제1쇄 발행
2008년 10월 20일 초판 제2쇄 발행

저자   김용구
발행인   이장연
발행처   도서출판 원
406-131 인천광역시 연수구 동춘동 794-2
국제법외교사자료실
전화 02) 584-3618
032) 831-5870
010-9386-1941, 010-5215-3617
팩시밀리 02) 584-3617
032) 831-5203

E-mail: kl5992@netsgo.com
yongkookim@hotmail.com

출판등록 제7호

ISBN 89-89443-05-9-03340

값 20,000 원